The Yukon
Hiking Guide

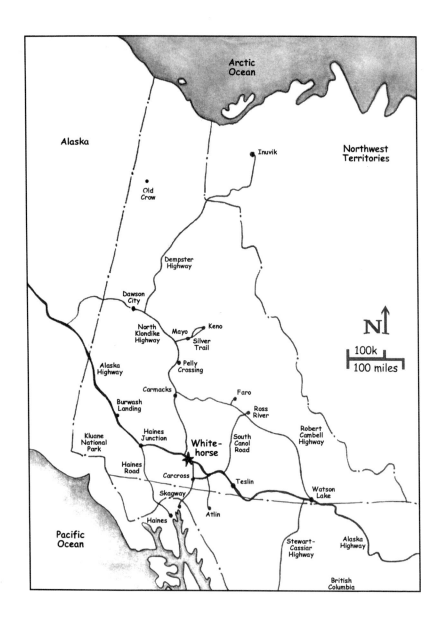

Arctic
Ocean

Alaska

Northwest
Territories

Inuvik

Old
Crow

Dempster
Highway

Dawson
City

North
Klondike
Highway

Mayo

Keno

Silver
Trail

Pelly
Crossing

Alaska
Highway

Carmacks

Faro

Burwash
Landing

Ross
River

Kluane
National
Park

Haines
Junction

White-
horse

South
Canol
Road

Robert
Cambell
Highway

Haines
Road

Carcross

Teslin

Watson
Lake

Skagway

Atlin

Pacific
Ocean

Haines

Stewart-
Cassiar
Highway

Alaska
Highway

British
Columbia

N

100k
100 miles

The Yukon Hiking Guide

Over 100 Walks, Hikes and Treks

Design and Layout: Curtis Vos and Derek Jamensky.
File preparation by Instant Computer Services.
Printed in Vancouver by Mitchell Press.

Published by Borealis Books, Whitehorse, Yukon. Ordering: YH6 box 4614, Whitehorse, YT, Y1A-2R8 (867) 668-2405 curtisvos@hotmail.com

Canadian Cataloging in Publication Data
Vos, Curtis 1968-
TheYukon Hiking Guide
ISBN 0-9686627-0-6

1. Hiking-Yukon Territory–Guidebooks   2. Trails–Yukon Territory–Guidebooks 3. Yukon Territory–Guidebooks. I. Title
GV199.44.C22Y8 2000   796.51'09719'1   C00-900133-6

Acknowledgments: I would first like to thank my family and friends for all of their support throughout this exhaustive project. Without the help of my parents, Walter and Lorraine, this book would not have been published. My brother Ed loves visiting the North and a number of his photographs are found in these pages.
The following businesses shared time and resources; their support was invaluable. Macs Fireweed (especially Lise Schonewille), Photo Vision Yukon, Coast Mountain Sports, Valhalla Sports, Lost Moose Publishing and Flash Mountain Bikes/ Atlin Happy Trails.
For editing assistance I extend warm thanks to Walter Vos, Lori Kond, Jack Schick and Afan Jones. Bruce Bennett, Todd Powell, Charles Jurasz, and Dave Watt have also assisted with tips and hiking information. Big thanks to the Yukon Conservation Society and especially Rosa Brown for assistance.
Thanks go out to my friends in the Yukon and down south for lending a hand on trail research and feedback, sharing (or covering!) gas and food expenses. It's been a pleasure to share the trails with you.
Lastly, I owe a debt of gratitude to a number of local hiking guides that I have enjoyed using over the years: Whitehorse Hikes and Bikes, The Kluane National Park Hiking Guide and Along the Dempster.

Introduction 8
How to use this guide 10

CHAPTER 1: THE LAND AND ITS INHABITANTS

The Yukon 14
The Land 15
The Water 16
The Sky 17
The Plants 18
The Fish 20
The Birds 21
The Mammals 22
First Nations 24
The Klondike Goldrush 28
The Yukon Today 30

CHAPTER 2: INTO THE OUTDOORS

Trip Planning 32
Gear and Supplies 34
Staying Found 36
Interacting with the Environment 38
Bears 40
Advanced Travel Tips 42
(Very) Basic First Aid 43
Summer Sports 44
Winter Sports 48
Advanced Hikes 50

CHAPTER 3: WHITEHORSE REGION

1. Watson Lake Walks 54
2. Mount White 56
3. Monarch Mountain 58
4. Whitehorse Walks 60
5. Miles Canyon 62
6. Grey Mountain Trails 64
7. Whitehorse Lakes 66
8. Ibex Valley 68
9. Fish Lake Area 70
10. Mount Lorne 74
11. Carcross Walks 76
12. Mount Montana 78
13. Feather Peak 80
14. Dewey Lakes 82
15. Chilkoot Pass 84

CHAPTER 4: KLUANE/CHILKAT REGION

16. Mount Ripley 92
17. Mount Ripinski 94
18. Chilkat Pass 96
19. Samuel Glacier 98
20. South Kluane Park 100
21. Cottonwood Trails 102
22. King's Throne 106
23. Auriol Trail 108
24. Haines Junction Walks 110
25. Mount Decoeli 112
26. Slims River Valley 114
27. Sheep Mountain Area 118
28. Kluane Lake 120
29. Burwash LooP 122

CHAPTER 5: CENTRAL AND NORTHERN YUKON

30. Carmacks Walks 130
31. Carmacks Agate/ Gem Trails .132
32. Faro Trails 134
33. Mount Haldane 136
34. Keno Trails 138
35. Ridge Road Heritage Trail 140
36. Dawson City Walks 142
37. Midnight Dome 144
38. Mount Monolith Viewpoint 146
39. Tombstone Pass 148
40. Blueberry Hill 150
41. North Fork Pass 152
42. Mount Distincta 156
43. Sapper Hill 158
44. Arctic Circle 160

CHAPTER 6: TRAVEL INFORMATION

Roads and Highways 165
Communities 166
Campgrounds 169
Parks and Protected Areas 172
Conservation 173
Travel Information 174
Contact Numbers 175
Recommended Reading 176
Glossary 178
First Nations Place Names 179
Index 180

INTRODUCTION

Finally, a hiking guide that covers the entire Yukon Territory and beyond. This comprehensive guide offers trails and routes for all ages and interests. It is useful for trip planning as well as a valuable field resource.

The Yukon Hiking Guide, with more than one hundred walks and hikes, is an excellent introduction to some of the finest hiking terrain in the world. Pure air and water, expansive vistas unmarred by development, low tree-lines and wildlife sightings are just a few of the reasons to experience the Yukon wilderness firsthand.

Before you head out, be aware that many of the areas described in this book are truly wild and rarely visited. Land, road and water features are in a constant state of change. Unlike southern trail systems, many trails and even trailheads are not marked and park rangers may not be available for help.

This guide is no substitute for experience and common sense, and the author cannot be held responsible for any difficulties encountered while using this book. If any erroneous information is detected, please contact me for use in subsequent printings. In addition, be aware that the Yukon is bear country and prepare accordingly to avoid any problems.

While writing this guide I've come to realize all the different ways people interact with nature. It may be adrenalin-oriented recreation, a peaceful escape from busy schedules, social bonding, wildlife viewing, spirituality or sustenance. Whatever your choice of activity, practice low-impact travel and camping so that future travelers will experience the land as pure and undisturbed as you have. In addition, please respect people's livelihood choices (i.e. trappers, miners), First Nations land, resources and artifacts, as well as private property.

This guidebook is the culmination of thousands of hours of wilderness travel. During that time I have seen almost every mammal found in the Territory and have been literally moved to tears on the tops of rugged mountains overlooking the world. The chance to listen to the sound of silence, to gaze over a land completely untouched by 'progress', to feel a calmness that comes from experiencing a sense of oneness with nature, this is the magic of pure wilderness.

As the world gets more and more fragmented due to the unrelenting alteration and destruction of habitats, the need to protect intact eco-systems like the ones found in the Yukon take on a special urgency.
A number of excellent conservation groups are found in the Yukon and are listed on page 173. Let us all do our part to preserve this great land, a natural heritage bequeathed to all creatures, big and small.

Happy Trails!
Curtis Vos
Whitehorse, Yukon

HOW TO USE THIS GUIDE

I have personally walked every hike and option in this guide, with a few exceptions; in those cases written material and firsthand accounts were used and are noted accordingly. Every effort was made to ensure accurate logistics; be flexible as your own experiences may vary.

Be aware of the distinction between trails, roads and routes. Trails indicate an established or semi-established foot trail, and roads are often undrivable access roads. Routes often have some puzzling sections and are usually recommended only for the experienced backcountry traveler prepared with a topographical map and the knowledge of how to use it.

Finally, for extended trips, remember to be completely self-sufficient as help may be days away. I highly recommend a careful study of Chapter 2 for trip planning as well as for general interest.

Planning a Hike: This book is designed to have something for all tastes and interests. Many **Easy** and **Medium** trails are found around the communities and are great for moderate nature walks. Most have interpretive signs, maps found at the trailheads, and are well within the range of most people.

Medium/ Hard and **Hard** hikes usually involve some substantial elevation gains, tricky terrain, creek crossings and possible routefinding.

Very Hard hikes can be just below 'technical' mountaineering and are therefore recommended for experienced backcountry and alpine travelers only. Map reading skills and sound judgment are required.

Distances: All distances are return unless otherwise noted.

Time: This is based on an average fitness level. I recommend budgeting more time for fun and safety.

Elev. gain: The maximum elevation gain encountered during the hike.

Season: This is an approximation based on experience, the general climate of the area and elevation. It may vary considerably from year to year.

MERITS: Showcases some of the best features of the hike.

CONCERNS: Safety, comfort and low environmental impact tips.

Conversion: Both metric and imperial measurements are used in this guide. For distances, kilometres (km) are used. For conversion purposes, remember that 1 mile equals 1.6 km, and 3 miles roughly equal 5 km. Elevations are measured in feet as this is common on most topographical maps. To convert feet to metres, simply multiply the number by three; 3 feet roughly equals 1 metre (M).

Maps: The hand-drawn maps in this guide are intended as a simplified overview of the hikes. For many hikes they are sufficient, but lack scope and detail for more advanced hikes as well as most of the options. Check out the first instruction box at the start of each hike to see if a government issue topographical map is recommended.

All maps are 1:50,000 Canadian Topographical maps unless otherwise noted. Maps are listed as **Interest Only** (not necessary), **Useful** (handy, good for options) or **Recommended** (very important). Topographical maps are generally recommended for options.

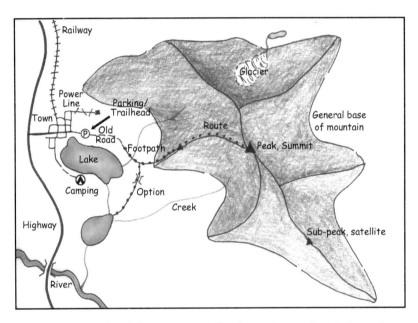

Terminology: The following specialized words are found throughout the guide:

Buckbrush: Large shrubs like willow, dwarf birch and alder.

Bushwack: To travel off trail through vegetation, usually buckbrush.

Cirque: Bowl-shaped, possibly glaciated, depression high in a mountain.

Interpreted: Usually means interpretive signs can be found along trail.

Pass: A small or large opening in a mountain ridge or range.

Scrambling: Hiking with your hands.

Sidehill: To hike on steep slopes, often around lesser peaks.

Trailhead: The start and/or end of a hike, sometimes marked by a sign.

CHAPTER 1

THE LAND
AND ITS INHABITANTS

THE YUKON

The Yukon Territory, found in the north west corner of Canada, is a land of vast and unique wilderness. Few places on earth harbour such unspoiled wildlands and such interesting human history.

Canada's highest mountains are found in Kluane National Park which is part of the largest non-polar icefield in the world. The Yukon, known as the 'Land of the Midnight Sun', has a sky which is often painted with dramatic cloudscapes or the truly magical Aurora Borealis.

The Yukon is home to more than one thousand species of plants, almost thirty types of fish, over two hundred kinds of birds, and sixty two species of mammals. Wildlife sightings, far from uncommon, are often the most treasured memories of a trip into the Yukon wilds.

The human history of the Yukon is similarly rich and diverse. The Territory's first people arrived tens of thousands of years ago. They established complex trading alliances and lived a semi-nomadic life of hunting, fishing and gathering. The character of the Yukon was dramatically altered with the arrival of tens of thousands of stampeders during the Klondike Gold Rush in 1898, the worlds most incredible mineral rush.

Today the Yukon is home to just over thirty thousand people, about the same as one hundred years ago. Though modern amenities are available, the communities still maintain a distinctively northern flavour.

The Yukon, larger than California but with about one thousandth of its population, is a land largely untouched by modern despoilment. Due to the long daylight hours, the low treeline, the abundant wildlife and the magnificent views, the Yukon is truly a backpacker's paradise.

THE LAND

Two great land masses comprise the Territory and are generally split by the Tintina trench. This division flows northwest through Ross River, Faro, Stewart Crossing and Dawson City. Mountains and land to the North of this line are primarily sedimentary rocks like limestone and sandstone. This terrain is part of what is known as original North America.

Over the course of millions of years, plate tectonics caused land masses to crash into the former coast, shaping the spectacular Coast and Saint Elias Ranges of today. This area, lying to the south of the Tintina, particularly Kluane National Park, has a great variety of rocks and minerals.

Mountains and Ranges: The coastal ranges to the south are heavily glaciated, in particular the Saint Elias Range in Kluane National Park. The peaks found in the park, like Mount Logan (19,550 feet), Mount Saint Elias (18,000 feet) and Mount Lucania (17,250 feet) are Canada's highest. All three mountains, despite their enormity, are rarely seen giants, frequently hiding themselves in swirling blankets of clouds.

Mount Logan, in particular, is a fascinating mountain. Considered the largest mountain in the world, it has a plateau almost the size of Manhattan Island and a vertical relief of over 13,000 feet!

Ancient ranges in the north, with their low or non existent treeline and crumbly summits, have what may be best described as a medieval flavour. The South Ogilvie Range, found along the Dempster Highway, bears the effects of the last ice age while the North Ogilvie Range largely missed it.

Rocks and Minerals: The quest for golden wealth has caught the attention of many a recent traveller to these lands. "Placer" gold, for which the Klondike region is famous, has been liberated by water and redeposited in gravel. Some areas of the Klondike have been gone over three or more times and still produce the beloved metal. Visitors are sure to encounter numerous commercial gold panning stands. While the findings are usually slim, it's always a delight to discover "colours" in the bottom of your pan.

In addition to gold deposits, silver, galena (lead ore), and zinc can be found in the territory. Many beautiful rocks can be found along the creeks and rocky ridges of Kluane National Park. Look for (but do not collect) petrified wood, marine fossils and conglomerates. The Carmacks area has a number of agate (quartz) and gem trails (page 132). Ancient colourful rocks and "thundereggs" (concretions) can be found in the ranges along the Dempster Highway.

THE WATER

Rivers: From looking at Yukon maps, or from the air, the river systems look like a vast series of veins and arteries. The water nurtures the body of land as well as all the creatures living on it.

Most water in the Territory eventually flows into the Yukon River and is carried, via a very circuitous route, to the Pacific Ocean. More than seventy major rivers join the mighty Yukon along its relentless journey. Water in the Liard Basin, near Watson Lake, flows into the Mackenzie River as does the massive Peel River drainage. Ice melting in southern Kluane Park feeds the mighty Tatshenshini and Alsek rivers which course tumultuously towards the Pacific.

Lakes: The largest lake in the Yukon is the aquamarine-coloured Kluane Lake, which is found on the edge of the Park. The Dezadeash, Aishihik and Kusawa Lakes, also seen in this general area, are big, beautiful and mountain-fringed.

South and east of Whitehorse the deep waters of the Southern Lakes System (Tutshi, Bennett, Marsh, Tagish) can be discovered. Atlin Lake, just south of the Yukon border, is British Columbia's largest freshwater lake. Lake Laberge, immortalized in the verse of Robert Service, lies to the north of Whitehorse.

Smaller and shallower lakes are found throughout the Territory. Look for marl, a mixture of various sedimentary materials, and loess, a glacial dust. Both materials color the waters vivid shades of emerald and turquoise.

Snow and Ice: Snow begins to dust the mountaintops as early as the end of August. It can take one to two months for it to move down to the valleys. The Yukon generally gets very little snow in the winter due to the rain shadow effect of the Coastal Range. The snow is usually dry and sugary, and can be great for cross-country skiing. Late snow can be found in the higher mountains all summer long until the cycle begins again.

Glaciation occurs when snow fails to melt in the summer months. Snow crystals break down into ice and form glaciers. Over time the weight of the ice begins to be pulled downward by gravity. The ice scoops and grinds the land resulting in a number of unique topographical features. Kluane National Park, where the last ice age is alive and well, is one of the finest places to see the processes of glaciation and erosion. Enormous glaciers, some up to 80 kilometers long, like the Kaskawulsh, Lowell, Donjek and Klutlan, dominate valleys and have to be seen to be believed.

THE SKY

The Midnight Sun provides seemingly endless days in mid-summer and adds an unmistakable quality to northern summers. The longest day of the year is June 21 (Summer Solstice) and is celebrated in many parts of the Yukon, especially in Dawson. The Dempster Highway north of the Arctic Circle and Inuvik are some of the best places to experience sun on your face, long after midnight.

Clouds: The clouds found in the Yukon are frequently spectacular. Look for Mares Tails, high wispy clouds covering the high portion of the sky. Lenticular clouds look like giant cotton spaceships and are found orbiting around the mountains. Mackerel Sky around sunset or sunrise often catches some of the most colourful rays of the sun. Rolling bands of Cumulus are common and can be seen rippling back into distant horizons.

Northern Lights: The Northern Lights are shimmering bands of neon-like light known scientifically as the Aurora Borealis. The lights are caused by subatomic particles in the upper atmosphere drawn to the magnetic poles. They can occur any time of year but are scarcely visible from May to the end of July. The Northern Lights occur simultaneously around the south pole and are known as the Aurora Australis.
The auroras are tied in with solar flare activity and generally follow an eleven year cycle; they are peaking from 1999-2002.
The best displays are often found around midnight on clear, crisp nights. For good viewing, dress warmly and get away from artificial light if possible. To photograph the lights, use a tripod and a fast film (400 ASA or more). Try an exposure time of 2 to 6 seconds and an aperture of F1.4 or F2.

The Night Sky: Due to the long daylight hours the night sky is not seen for up to 3 months in summer. Occasionally the Big Dipper can be seen (see page 37) as well as the Summer Triangle. Once into August, the stars return and the Persied Meteor Shower of August 11-13 is well worth planning for.
Due to the small amount of light pollution, the Yukon can be a wonderful place to star gaze in the fall, winter and spring. Look for Orion, the Hunter, and the brightest star, Sirius (the Dog star), shimmering in the evening sky. Binoculars are an excellent tool for getting a closer look at stars, planets, and other celestial objects.

THE PLANTS

Northern Forests: The Yukon forest is classified as Northern Boreal. Characteristics include stands of primarily coniferous trees like black and white spruce, and lodgepole pine. Trembling aspen and balsam poplar are found in young and mixed forests. Several types of willow, alder and dwarf birch comprise much of the shrubbery.

With long, cold winters as well as a constantly frozen ground (permafrost) in many areas, the Yukon is not an easy place to be a tree. Look for "drunken forests", stands of twisted black spruce growing on permafrost and leaning madly in all directions. Trees are commonly much older than they look; the small, stunted spruce that you see by the road may have been a seedling when the Titanic sailed.

Understanding forest dynamics is no easy task. A complex universe of interaction is happening below the surface and in the air of a typical forest. Material is constantly being reused and recycled by fires, bacteria, fungi, plants and animals.

Autumn in the Yukon is a visual treat as the forest and tundra erupt into colour. Hiking during this season, usually late August to mid September, can be cool and wet but highly memorable.

Forest Fires: While fires have the potential to destroy entire communities, they are often as natural as rain and snow. Usually a mature forest, dominated by stands of older conifers, burns and the cycle starts again. Burned ground can provide excellent habitat for a range of life. The aptly named fireweed (below), official flower of the Yukon, is one of the first colonizers. The gourmet morel mushroom also blooms in a first year burn. Hare, lynx and moose are all quick to move in to burn sites to graze or hunt.

As the years pass, aspen and occasionally pine establish themselves, later to be replaced by spruce. As these trees grow to maturity, the forest is once again primed for a fire.

NOTE: Yukon forest fires are commonly caused by lightning strikes. However, in recent years the percentage of human-started fires has grown considerably. Please respect 'no burn' times, put fires dead out, and report any new fires.

Habitat: Habitat recognition is very valuable when looking for particular plants. For example wild sage, juniper and the purple pentstemon flower can all be found on dry south-facing hills and mountains. The brief, alpine summer above the treeline produces intricate and brightly-coloured flowers like moss campion and wolly lousewort. Wetter forested areas contain cottongrass, cloudberries and numerous shrubs. Drier forests are home to colourful wildflowers like wild rose, lupines and bluebells. Bunchberry and kinnikinnick provide some of the ground-cover. Finally, disturbed ground like forest burns and old roads are home to a variety of attractive flowers and mushrooms.

Wildflowers and Other Plants: The Yukon can be a very colorful place when the wildflowers begin to bloom. The prairie crocus heralds the start of spring and is followed by the many varieties of vetch which provide a vibrant margin to northern highways. Fireweed blooms brilliantly mid-summer and often dominates huge areas.
Also look for Labrador tea and soapberry, common shrubs in many areas. Sedges, grasses, mosses and avens comprise much of the ground cover. A close look at the tundra (treeless zone) will reveal an intricate mosaic of life. Otherworldly mushrooms are found during wetter summers. Lichens, some several hundred years old, weave intricate patterns on rocks and trees.

Useful and Edible Plants: Local First Nations people have long known the value of the plant kingdom for medicinal, nutritional and practical use. Numerous plants can be gathered to make teas, oils, potpourris, jams, medicines, poultices and much more. Acquiring this practical knowledge is a great way to reacquaint oneself with nature.
Wild foods can be the best the world has to offer. They are fresh, organic, unpackaged, non-transported and FREE! Tasty wild berries include raspberries, strawberries, cloudberries, blueberries and cranberries. Fungi fanatics will surely enjoy the shaggy manes, bolete, puffballs and, best of all, the morel mushrooms which can all be found in damper summers. Numerous greens, like fireweed and dandelion shoots, make an excellent addition to salads.
NOTE: Be positive in your identification of any wild food; many excellent guidebooks are available. Remember to eat a small amount of any wild food to begin with. Wild mushrooms should always be cooked and never combined with alcohol. One final note: please don't clear-cut any patch of wild food, gather far from established trails and be aware of berry-loving bears.

THE FISH

Salmon: There are five types of salmon that travel the Yukon waterways: chum, coho, chinook (a.k.a. king), sockeye and kokanee. The movements and numbers of these fish often confound fish biologists and their numbers are presently quite precarious.

Large Freshwater Fish: Arctic grayling (see sketch) are common in many rivers. Three trout varieties (lake, rainbow and dolly varden) are found in the lakes and are very tasty. Northern pike (a.k.a. jackfish, swamp shark) and four types of whitefish (broad, lake, pygmy and round) also inhabit the lakes. Mysterious fish like the burbot and innconu are occasionally taken by anglers.

Wee Fish: Small fish in the Yukon are endowed with some delightfully silly names like the ninespine stickleback, boreal smelt, lake chub, and of course the slimy sculpins. These little fish play an important role in aquatic bio-systems.

The Arctic Grayling is a common Yukon fish found in many rivers and lakes. The grayling's large dorsal fin gives it its unique appearance.

Fishing and Fishwatching: Anglers will need an angling license. These can be purchased at a number of locations. In addition, see page 39 for more information on fishing. Consider visiting the Whitehorse Fishladder (page 61) during mid-summer for possible sightings of salmon and other fish. Contact Renewable Resources (page 173) for a free booklet on the location of stocked lakes in the Yukon, as well as a free guided tour of the Chinook Salmon run along Wolf Creek, near Whitehorse.

THE BIRDS

Birds of Prey: The bald eagle and golden eagle are commonly seen in most parts of the Territory. Owls are more often heard than seen, and varieties of falcons (like peregrines and gyrfalcons) and hawks (like sharp-shinned and the northern goshawk) fly pirouettes in the sky on their constant search for prey. Hikers should be cautious around cliffs so as not to disturb nesting areas.

Water Birds: Springtime is an excellent time to view migrating water birds especially in a canoe or kayak. Tundra and trumpeter swans spend part of spring at Swan Haven, 20 km from Whitehorse. (Contact Renewable Resources, page 173 for free tours). Floating birds like loons, grebes, geese, teals and mergansers all call the Yukon home for the summer.
Gulls and terns are common around water bodies, and over 20 species of sandpipers can be heard making a commotion along sandy beach fronts. A visit from a belted kingfisher (see the back of the Canadian 5 dollar bill) is always welcome. The plaintive cry of the pacific loon is both beautiful and haunting.

Forest and Field Birds: Many varieties of songbirds can be heard singing during the long summer mornings. Sparrows, juncos, and other small birds can be spotted in forest and field during their busy day of bug and seed collecting. Several species of woodpeckers send staccato signals through the forest. The four types of grouse are commonly seen and can easily startle an unwary traveler.
The ptarmigan, a close relative of the grouse, is frequently seen and heard in the sub-alpine and tundra. The ubiquitous raven is seen in virtually every corner of the Yukon as well as its cousins, the grey jay and the magpie. Also look for barn and cliff swallows who perform amazing aerial acrobatics.

A Grouse, a.k.a. Yukon Chicken, thinking that it is cleverly hidden.

THE MAMMALS

History: Like the people of the north,many of the animals found today are pioneers from another time and place. Carmacks represents the southernmost extension of Beringia, a former refuge for giant ice age beasts. Mastodons, giant sloths, short-faced bears, scimitar cats, and a 600 pound beaver (!) all roamed these verdant valleys. These species were unable to survive the passage of time while other Beringia era animals like the caribou, wood bison, moose and wolf thrive to this day. The land's first human inhabitants, who arrived late in Beringian history, also managed to outlast this transitional period.

Since the ice age, numerous other species have made their way up to the north from southern climes. In just the last century the mule deer, white-tailed deer and the coyote, have visited the Yukon and decided to stay. The rarely seen cougar, which considers deer quite delectable, is the latest newcomer to these lands.

Habitat: A healthy habitat is crucial for any living thing. This applies especially for far-ranging animals like bears and caribou. Sheep and other ungulates (hoofed animals) are heavily dependent on salt and mineral licks. Safe birthing and wintering grounds are also a critical requirement.

While in the past century, overhunting and road access have impacted a number of species, the chances of seeing wildlife are very good.

Cycles: The numbers of grazing herd animals, like barrenground caribou, rise and fall according to how much their habitat can sustain them. Predators closely follow the cycles of their prey.

For example, every seven to ten years the population of snowshoe hares builds to a climax. The lynx, who eat an almost exclusive diet of hare, than begin to have larger and healthier litters. This continues for several years until the number of hares drops, followed by a steep decline in the lynx population.

The elusive Wolverine is an excellent indicator of a healthy ecosystem.

Small Mammals: Arctic ground squirrels and red squirrels are very common as well as the ubiquitous snowshoe hare. Mice, voles, shrews scurry in the shadows of rocks and forests, and the little brown bat is found in a number of Yukon batcaves. Shrieking marmots and pikas are found in the alpine zone, the waddling beaver and porcupine in the lower wet lands.

Large Mammals: The list below shows 1997 estimates of animal numbers from the Yukon Bureau of Statistics. Omitted from this chart are the cats, the lynx, and the cougar (a.k.a. mountain lion) as well as some of the dogs (coyotes, red fox). Both the Pacific and Arctic Oceans are home to a wide variety of aquatic mammals like whales and seals.

Mammal:	Pop:	Page:	Distribution:
Grizzly Bear	6,500	Page 41	Entire Yukon
Black Bear	10,000	Page 41	Entire Yukon
Wolf	4,500		Entire Yukon
Moose	55,000	Page 101	Entire Yukon
Woodland Caribou	32,000		South and central Yukon
Barrenground Caribou	245,000		Northern Yukon
Elk (Wapiti)	100		South and central Yukon
Dall Sheep	19,000	See below	Most of Yukon
Stone Sheep	3,000		Southeast, central Yukon
Mountain Goat	2,000	Page 57	South Yukon

Dall Sheep in Kluane National Park.

FIRST NATIONS

Han

Dene

Gw'itchin

Han

Upper Tanana

Northern Tutchone

Kaska women from Mayo

Southern Tutchone

Inland Tlingit

Kaska

Tagish

Tlingit

This map shows approximate historical lands of the various Yukon and area First Nations. There is alot of overlap.

"Chilkoot Jack" of the Tlingit

Many **Kaska** today live a life close to the land and use their own language more than any other Yukon First Nations. Stick Gambling, drumming, and the telling of legends are ways that the Kaska use to blend the past with the present.

The **Inland Tlingit** are related to many of the Coastal native peoples (Haida, Salish) and produce the distinctive embroidered clothing, ceremonial masks and architecture that is famous worldwide. Tlingit language was the language of business as they traveled and traded with the numerous bands in the interior Yukon. The Chilkoot and Chilkat Passes were original trade-routes of the Tlingit and were jealously guarded by them.

The **Tagish** have traditionally lived throughout the Southern Lakes system. They traded with the interior and coastal peoples, eventually linking closely with the Tlingit. "Skookum" Jim, "Tagish" (or "Dawson") Charlie and Kate Carmacks of this area helped discover the rich Klondike goldfields.

The **Tutchone** have always called the central Yukon home, living in the region bordered by the icy Coastal ranges to the south and the Ogilvie/Selwyn ranges to the North. **Southern Tutchone** traded regularly with the Tlingit and were deeply impacted by the building of the Alaska Highway in the late nineteen forties. **Northern Tutchone** live north of Lake Laberge and speak slightly different dialects.

The **Han,** who presently live near Dawson, are also known as the **Tr'ondek Hwech'in.** They have traditionally depended on the rich, oily salmon as a major part of their diet. Over the past two centuries the Han have had to deal with the many traders, prospectors and miners visiting and settling on their traditional lands. Today the Han straddle an international border with members in Dawson, Yukon, and Eagle, Alaska.

The **Gwich' in**, have worked together for millennia to fish the local rivers or hunt the migrating Porcupine caribou herd, a mainstay of their diet to this day. Recent digs in the nearby Bluefish Caves suggest an occupancy in the area of up to thirty thousand years.

The **Upper Tanana** have territory in the Yukon and Alaska and are closely related to the Han. They are the smallest band in the Territory with just under one hundred and fifty members.

History: According to the scientific view pioneers from Asia began to populate the Americas between 25,000 and 40,000 years ago by crossing the Bering Land Bridge. This strip of land, now submerged, was caused by extensive glaciation that lowered water levels in the area. Native history often differs from this scientific view with occupation dating much further back. Irregardless, these early people lived in a fascinating and harsh land of exotic Beringinan animals (like the wooly mammoth), and green, rolling hills that were literally walled in by enormous glacial ice caps. Their hardiness and adaptability paid off as they outlived many of the animals of this era. (Those interested in this period should check out the Beringia Centre in Whitehorse).

The original people of these lands largely lived a semi-nomadic lifestyle of hunting, fishing and gathering plants. Semi permanent meat drying camps were often used with food cached along common travel routes. Northern Athapaskan Indians were a true example of an egalitarian (equal status) society with leadership depending on the nature of the activity. Intricate trade relations, inter-marrying and occasionally war, took place between neighboring tribes.

Lineage's were often passed through mothers and most families were divided into either Wolf or Crow. A range of rites of passage existed for both adolescent boys and girls. Marriages were often arranged with special consideration to establishing ties between clans and tribes.

The Yukon's indigenous people have always shared a complex storytelling tradition and rich mythology very much connected to the ecology of the region. Shamans were found in many most tribes and served as important intermediaries to the Spirit world.

The arrival of Europeans, like in other areas of the Americas, led to an immense disturbance of traditional lifestyles. Certain trade goods like guns and metalwork may have eased life in some ways, but the greed, diseases and cultural indifference of many Europeans caused immeasurable upset. In addition, some local wildlife populations suffered a steep decline in numbers, affecting First Nations' autonomy. The influx of traders and miners also impacted traditional hunting and fishing camps; displacement of entire settlements was not uncommon.

Today, 'Land Claims' and 'Self Government' talks are beginning to make a positive change in the future of Yukon First Nations. Traditional events like storytelling and "potlatches" connect the past to the future and are common during the summer throughout the Territory. Dancing, music, arts, crafts and sporting events like the Arctic Winter Games display the richness of northern Aboriginal culture.

Public Access to Settlement Land: According to the Yukon Umbrella Final Agreement the public has a general right of access, without the consent of the affected First Nations, to enter, cross and stay on Undeveloped Settlement Land for a reasonable period of time for all non-commercial recreational purposes. In addition to this I would add the following: Never tamper with trapping and fishing equipment, cache and tent poles (long pointed poles often found in sub alpine areas), buildings and structures. Never remove any historic artifact from its location. You may wish to report any findings to the nearest First Nations. Most communities have administration offices, which may be contacted for any questions regarding land use, place names, historical information and current events.

Language and Place Names: The Yukon First Nations, with the exception of the Inland Tlingit, belong to the Athapaskan language group. Other members of this language group include the Dene of the Northwest Territories/Nunavut as well as many of the indigenous peoples of the southwestern United States.

Although many elders are fluent in their mother tongue, native languages are threatened. These elders, linguists, and a proud minority of youth are working to preserve this essential aspect of their culture.

Many of the names of the mountains, lakes and rivers in this guide are of native origin and often convey a more intimate knowledge of the land. Some translations are found in the text or in the glossary on page 178. Those desiring to learn more about First Nations culture may wish to check out the Native Interpretive Centres in Dawson, Carmacks and Pelly Crossing. In addition, museums in Whitehorse, Teslin and Burwash Landing have many interesting Native displays and attractions.

Jean Cambell Collection

Tlingit with ceremonial clothing.

- 27 -

THE KLONDIKE GOLDRUSH

Discovery Day: Prospectors and fur traders began to trickle into the north during the 1800's. Some workable areas were found and small towns sprang up along the banks of the Yukon river. The drive to find the "Eldorado", the legendary motherlode of gold, was on every prospector's mind. In the summer of 1896 that goal was to be realized. "Skookum" Jim, "Tagish Charlie" and "Lyin'" George Carmacks were hunting moose along Rabbit Creek, a tributary of the Thron-diuck (Klondike) River on August 16, testing the streams occasionally for gold deposits. No one is positive about who found the gold first and it matters little. The swampy area surrounding the creek, since renamed Bonanza, and its tributary Eldorado, would yield the highest concentration of gold ever discovered.

The Rush Begins: Due to the remote location of the Klondike goldfields it would be almost a year after the big discovery before the outside world found out about the rich goldfields of the Klondike. Much of North America was in an economic depression and the public was captivated by the adventurous appeal of a trip to a land where gold lay 'thick as cheese'.

It is said that over a million people planned to head for the strike, with about one hundred thousand seriously attempting it. Coastal towns like Seattle and Vancouver boomed as hordes of goldseekers rushed through, dropping small fortunes to outfit themselves for the Klondike. There were about half a dozen routes to the Yukon; most of these required traveling partly by water.

Probably the most compelling image of the gold rush is the line of stampeders hiking the Chilkoot Pass in the dead of winter. One can only imagine the fortitude necessary to shuttle the required thousand pounds of food over the icy pass well renowned for its large volume of snow and blasting coastal winds.

Nonetheless, by spring thousands of eager men and women lined Lake Bennett, building ships and readying themselves for the thousand kilometer float trip down river to Dawson. Fearsome rapids like the Whitehorse and Five Finger Rapids plagued the ragged army of hopeful adventurers en-route to the 'City of Gold'.

Bill Roozeman Collection

A portion of the armada of over seven thousand boats that left the shores of Lake Bennett in spring of 1898.

Dawson City: Dawson City, found at the swampy confluence of the Klondike and Yukon Rivers, boomed in the years following the discovery. Wall tents (canvas mainstays of the northern traveler), cabins and false-fronted buildings popped up like mushrooms.

Much to the chagrin of the stampeders, the rich ground was already staked and for many the rush was a bust. Those who went north anticipating shortages in Dawson and those with valuable services to offer were the real winners of this mad race.

The wild town filled with eccentrics, entrepreneurs, song girls, prostitutes, poets, renegades, and mounties. The North West Mounted Police, led by the legendary Samuel Bennifield Steele, kept an eye on the flood of "chee-chakos" (newcomers). Their strict gun laws undoubtedly prevented much heartache and bloodshed. Doctors, nurses, nuns and priests also arrived with the rush and soon administered to the burgeoning population of scurvy and tuberculosis victims.

In 1899 a discovery in Nome, Alaska, sent thousands packing, and Dawson City became somewhat more civilized with a decidedly Victorian feel. Giant dredges moved into the Klondike altering the landscape in a dramatic and destructive way.

Dawson City has gone through several more booms and busts over the past century. Today the "city" has a population of about 2500, and an economy based primarily on tourism. The history of the world's greatest gold rush lingers on in the colourful town and in the surrounding green and rolling hills.

THE YUKON TODAY

Other Rushes: The search for mineral wealth has shaped much of the recent history of the Yukon. During the Klondike Gold Rush, thousands of hopeful miners flooded into Atlin following a rich strike there. Less than a decade later, gold was found in present-day Kluane National Park. Although heavily mined, the returns were very disappointing. The Whitehorse Copper Belt and Mount Montana south of Whitehorse, also have a similar mining history of boom and bust.

In the 1920s silver ore was found in the Keno and Mayo area, creating these towns and the Silver Trail of today. The Faro mine opened in the late sixties and once provided up to one quarter of the world's lead supply! Lead is used for car batteries (among other uses) and it's safe to say that almost every city in the world has a little piece of Faro in it.

Economy: The cost of shipping and the competitive global market have reduced the amount of mining taking place in the Territory. Government services, (municipal, territorial and federal), employ up to five thousand local people annually. Tourism, particularly outdoor-related, is the fastest growing sector of the economy.

Ecology: Although the Yukon is sparsely populated, considerable environmental degradation has occurred over the past century. Numerous caribou herds and moose populations have shown a precipitous decline. Thousands of kilometers of roads have further fragmented wildlife populations.

Mining, while important to the ecomomy, has contributed to the compromising of a number of areas. While acknowledging that many trails in this guide are old mining roads, one can't help but think that many sites could have been cleaned up better, both for aesthetics and for the health of the immediate area. With activities like mining, logging and development there remains the usual battle between personal freedoms (economy) and collective responsibility (ecology). Bringing these two polarities into harmony is one of the great challenges of the new millenium.

People: In many ways the population of the Yukon today is a microcosm of Canada. First Nations have bands in every community in the Territory. Aside from native languages, accents from around the globe can be heard on Main Street, Whitehorse any day of the week. The redcoated Mounties celebrate their colourful history every summer. Local musicians and artists enrich the Yukon with their creativity. Scores of Yukoners participate in numerous running and biking races during the brief summer months.

CHAPTER 2

INTO THE OUTDOORS

TRIP PLANNING

Trip Planning: Good research and planning are the keys to back country safety, comfort and enjoyment. Be conservative with time and distances. Try to be flexible; it's the journey, not the destination, that really matters.

Smaller parties (2-6) are generally preferable to larger ones. Solo travel can be risky. Try to pick party members with similar goals, fitness levels and good communication skills. Always let someone reliable know where you're going and when you expect to return.

Safety: Remember that getting into trouble in the bush is usually due to a combination of factors. These are:
• Poor Planning: Inadequate research; inadequate resources like water, food, clothing, map and compass; lack of a back-up plan.
• Estimating: Overestimating experience and abilities; underestimating distances and terrain.
• Inattention: To route-finding and terrain, habitat, weather, nightfall, fatigue, hunger and dehydration.

General Comfort: A stretch before and after a good stiff hike is highly recommended. Massage (solo or duo) is another excellent choice for dealing with sore muscles.

Think ahead. If you are prone to back pains bring an extra sleeping pad. Get cold easy? Double up on insulation layers. Figuring out what to bring and what not to bring can be a real balancing act.

Doing a trip without a mishap, without forgetting something important, with perfect weather and conditions, rarely happens. A logical mind and a positive attitude can increase the chances of smooth back-country travel, which is truly heaven on earth.

Bugs: Mosquito populations can be moderate in many areas and relentless in others, but are generally not as severe as in many other places throughout Canada. Mosquito numbers usually peak mid-June to the end of July. Consider avoiding wet valley hikes (and parts of the Dempster highway) during this time. Exposed, windy areas, or near the banks of rushing rivers, can be good places for resting and camping during mosquito season.

Consider bringing insect repellent and possibly a bug hat and jacket. Wear bright clothing and try to avoid eating bananas. Mosquitos don't, however, like the smell of citrus fruits like oranges and grapefruit.

In addition, hornets, wasps and blackflies peak late summer. Pack a kit if you are allergic to stinging insects; use repellent for black flies.

Seasons: The seasons are loosely characterized as follows:
• Spring: Spring is cool and wet, as snow melts from the high grounds. It usually lasts from April to mid-May.
• Summer: Summer is fun, fast and furious. Nights can still be cool, but daytime highs can reach up to 30 degrees Celsius. Summer generally lasts from mid-May to late August. There is useable light for most of the night.
• Fall: Nights can be cool and wet, but the brilliant colors found in early fall make up for this discomfort. Fall usually lasts from late August to early-October.
• Winter: Winter is cold to very cold. The temperature can remain under 0 degrees Celsius (freezing) for several months at a time. It is, however, a dry cold and it is possible in most weather situations to properly dress for it. Winter lasts from about mid-October to April.

Weather: It is wise to be prepared for any type of weather any time of year; snow can fall even during summer months. Nonetheless, scorching hot days are common in this land of extremes.
Depending on the summer, it may rain very rarely or very consistently. The areas south of Whitehorse, especially the White and Chilkat (Haines) Passes, can receive heavy precipitation. There can be strong winds and white-outs in some mountainous areas. If lightning threatens, get off the mountain and away from tall trees and open areas.

Cloud Watching is a fun and practical activity. Although there is a saying in the Yukon that 'if you don't like the weather wait five minutes' an awarness of shifting weather conditions is very useful in mountainous country.
First off, those high, wispy and often spectacular clouds are known as cirrus or 'mares tails". Lots of these clouds usually mean a new weather system is coming in, often a rainy one. A sky filled with cottony clouds (cumulus) is usually a sign of fair weather and they are the best for lying back and picking forms out of. If they start to swell and fill much of the sky keep an eye out for storm clouds (cumulonimbus).
Clouds in the far southern Yukon and Alaska are often drizzle clouds like nimbus and stratus. Dont forget the raingear. Finally the clouds found in the middle layer of the sky (altocumulus, lenticular and altostratus may rise or fall according to the whims of nature. These clouds look fantastic lit up by the midnight sun.
Remember a knowledge of clouds can add comfort to a trip, dramatically improve photos and be a constant source of inspiration. Don't forget to look up!

GEAR AND SUPPLIES

Basics
- ☐ Map(s)
- ☐ Compass/ GPS
- ☐ Guidebook(s)
- ☐ Matches, lighter
- ☐ Water bottle(s)
- ☐ Pocket knife
- ☐ First Aid Kit
- ☐ Pack (Fanny,
- ☐ Day, Overnight)
- ☐ Walking stick, ski pole

Clothing
Head and Neck:
- ☐ Sun hat
- ☐ Sunglasses
- ☐ Toque
- ☐ Balaclava
- ☐ Scarf

Upper Body:
- ☐ Undershirt
- ☐ T-shirt(s)
- ☐ Sweater(s)
- ☐ Vest

Lower Body:
- ☐ Underwear
- ☐ Long-johns
- ☐ Pants, sweats
- ☐ Rain/wind pants

Feet and Hands:
- ☐ Running shoes
- ☐ Hiking boots
- ☐ Sandals
- ☐ Camp shoes
- ☐ Creek shoes
- ☐ Liner socks
- ☐ Gaiters
- ☐ Mitts, gloves

Food
Breakfast:
- ☐ Cereals
- ☐ Bannock mix
- ☐ Granola
- ☐ Milk Powder

Snacks:
- ☐ Crackers
- ☐ Breads, buns
- ☐ Cheese
- ☐ Peanut butter
- ☐ Fruit: fresh, dry
- ☐ Trail mix, nuts
- ☐ Bars:Fruit, power, chocolate

Dinner:
- ☐ Pre-pack meals
- ☐ Noodles
- ☐ Rice
- ☐ Potatoes
- ☐ Tinned food
- ☐ Seasonings
- ☐ Dessert

Drinks:
- ☐ Coffee, Tea
- ☐ Juice mix
- ☐ Hot chocolate

Cooking Gear
- ☐ Stove
- ☐ Fuel
- ☐ Bowls, cups
- ☐ Utensils
- ☐ Can Opener
- ☐ Spatula, Ladle
- ☐ Knife

Camping Gear
- ☐ Tent
- ☐ Tarp(s)
- ☐ Poles
- ☐ Pegs
- ☐ Ropes
- ☐ Sleeping Bag(s)
- ☐ Sleeping Pad

Personal Kit
- ☐ Sunscreen
- ☐ Toilet paper
- ☐ Toothbrush
- ☐ Toothpaste
- ☐ Glasses
- ☐ Bio-soap
- ☐ Insect repellent
- ☐ Feminine products

Fun Stuff
- ☐ Binoculars
- ☐ Camera, film
- ☐ Books
- ☐ Paper, pen
- ☐ Cards, games

Survival Kit
- ☐ Whistle
- ☐ Candles
- ☐ Space blanket
- ☐ Extra matches
- ☐ Power food

Water: Keeping hydrated is essential. Always carry more water than you think you'll need. One litre for half days and two for full day trips should do. Remember, late snow can often be added to existing water supplies.

Excellent spring water can be found up in the mountains. Be very discriminatory and avoid areas of heavy human or animal activity. If in doubt, purify water by boiling or putting it through a water filtration unit. Giardia, (a.k.a. Beaver Fever, a nasty parasite that can cause severe intestinal distress) is found in some Yukon waters.

Food: Carry a variety of high-energy foods and snack frequently. Think sweet and savory as well as lightweight and low smell (bears/ wildlife); see pages 38 and 40. Eat well a day or two before a challenging hike. In cold weather, a thermos or water-bottle filled with sweet tea or a hot, savory soup can do wonders for morale. For overnight trips try to reduce packaging and organize breakfast, snack and dinner bags. Don't forget the basics like salt, sugar, and cooking oil.

Clothing: It is possible to dress for any type of weather anytime. Plan ahead and consider the worst possible weather conditions. Always bring more clothes than you think you'll need. The layering system works well. Remember the following:
• Wicking: long underwear (tops and bottoms) for perspiration removal.
• Insulation: shirts, sweaters, vests, and long pants for warmth.
• Shell: windbreaker, rain and/or snow pants and jacket.
A toque (wool cap) is a great idea any time of the year, as are a pair of gloves, and lots of extra socks for overnight trips.

Traditional clothes, like those made from fur and wool, have stood the test of time. Many space-age fabrics like polypropylene, capilene and gore-tex are a little overpriced but work quite well. Avoid wearing cotton and denim as they provide little insulation when wet.

Footwear: For easy and medium hikes, running shoes are generally sufficient. Medium/hard, hard, and very hard hikes require sturdier footwear with good ankle support. Break in new boots prior to a long trip, and apply moleskin or ductape to 'hot spots' as soon as you feel them. Try to keep your feet as dry as possible. Light inner socks and thicker outer socks help prevent chafing and are generally more comfortable.

Consider bringing extra footwear for creek crossings (see page 42) and for around camp. Sandals or neoprene canoe booties are both excellent.

STAYING FOUND

Maps/Orienteering: Most of the trails in this guide are straight forward, while some require a comprehensive knowledge of mountain topography. Check the first box before each hike for map recommendations; addresses of map retailers can be found on page 175.

Having a compass and/or a G.P.S. (global positioning system: a hand-held, battery-operated device that uses satellite technology to pinpoint locations) is your best defense against getting lost. Remember however, that having the niftiest gadgets in the world won't do you any good if they are not used correctly.

The magnetic declination in the Yukon is around 30 degrees to the east. In other words, your compass will point to the magnetic pole which is located somewhere in the middle of the Arctic islands. Map north (a.k.a. true north), points toward the North Pole. Line up your compass and map to line up the red arrow with the north arrow. Shift the map and compass 30 degrees to your left. This is true north. **NOTE:** This information is only necessary on advanced hikes.

If you are new to topographical maps, the following chart may help. Remember, learning the language of maps can be fun and will increase your safety considerably.

Map size:	Covers:	Best for:
1:50,000	About 500 maps cover the Yukon	Best for hiking, general interest of area
1:250,000	About 50 maps cover the Yukon	Good overview, helpful but lacking finer details
1:500,000	2 maps cover the Yukon	Good value, general reference, not good for hiking
1:1,000,000	1 map covers the Yukon	Good value, makes a great poster!

Route-finding: More advanced hikes may require some route finding. The following are a few hard-learned tips:
• Pay attention to unusual landmarks and look back frequently.
• Always remember what direction the highway is and where you are parked.
• Be more safety conscious the further you get from the road.
• Know where north is and how it relates to your direction of travel.

Finding North: Below are three ways of finding north:
1) Late Snow. North can generally be found by studying the spring snow. The south faces of mountains tend to melt first, the north faces last.

2) Make a sundial. This is fun even if not needed. Plant a large, straight stick into the ground. Mark the tip of the shadow with a small stick or rock. Wait for about twenty minutes and mark the next shadow. Draw a line between the two points. The line points east from the first marking. Draw a perpendicular line to make a north/south axis.

3) The Pole Star (Polaris): This star is impossible to see during part of the summer, but this stellar trick can be invaluable the rest of the year. Locate the Big Dipper; it is in the sky year-round. Start on the handle of the 'pot' (see below) and follow it around to the last two stars (the pointers). These stars point at a medium brightness star which is Polaris. Draw a line straight down to the horizon from Polaris; this is true north. All stars rotate around the Pole Star. In other words if you were lying down on the North Pole, Polaris would always be found directly over-head in the middle of the sky.

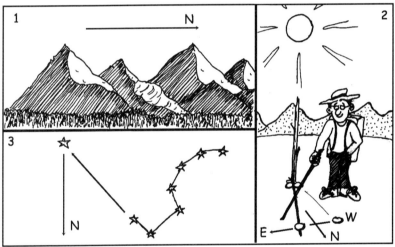

So you're lost . . . Getting lost can be a mild inconvenience or seriously life threatening. In all cases, stay calm, your mind is your greatest resource (or liability).

Whenever possible, try to find the point at which you first became dis-oriented. A little back tracking may be all that it takes.

If you must spend a night, collect enough wood to keep a good fire going. You will likely wake up regularly to stoke the fire. Use all of your gear to keep warm, utilize your backpack and every bit of clothing. Build a shelter and bedding from spruce bows if the weather is poor.

Remember that three of anything is a distress signal. Also consider tak-ing a communication device (radio, satellite phone) on advanced hikes.

INTERACTING WITH THE ENVIRONMENT

Low Impact Travel: Always show respect for the wilderness by being as low impact as possible. Remember to take out everything you bring in. For good karma points pack out any other trash as well. Leave excess packaging at home.

Become a trail steward; report unusual wildlife sightings, poachers, trail damage etc. Stick to established trails when possible and walk single file to avoid widening trails. Traveling on more gentle gradients causes less scaring; try to use boots with shallow treads.

When traveling off-trail, fan out to avoid damage to ground cover. Try to walk on more durable surfaces like rocks or late snow. Sod can be fairly durable; please avoid trashing moss and flower patches.

Low Impact Camping: Use existing campsites whenever possible or camp on durable surfaces. Avoid game trails, exposed, windy areas and places where water may collect. Pick a spot more than 200 feet from water and establish your cooking area downwind and at least 200 feet from your tent.

Avoid camp construction whenever possible, and give your camp a good 'once over' before leaving. Leaving an area that was home for a night or two in pristine condition should be a point of pride.

Fires, Cooking: Back-country stoves are almost always preferable to open fires as the Yukon can be a tinderbox in the summer. If you do need a fire, please use existing pits whenever possible. If no pits can be found build a fire on a sustainable surface like rocks, a beachfront or ideally make a 'mound fire'. Avoid making a fire in the tundra or on other vegetation where a fire scar may last for decades.

Use driftwood, or selectively harvest dead fall. The dry and dead lower branches of black spruce can be an excellent fire starter. Do not cut live trees or branches. Make sure your fire is totally out (cold to the touch), sift through for garbage and then scatter the ash and burnt rocks.

Waste: Avoid contaminating water sources. Wash yourself and your dishes at least several hundred feet away from your camp and always use biodegradable soap. Dispose of food wastes by packing it out, burning it, filtering through fine rocks or tossing it way out into a strong current. Never bury food or garbage.

If no outhouse exists do your business in a shallow hole or trench. Burn (if the ground is not too dry), bury or pack out your toilet paper and cover the hole with dirt, rocks and moss. A quick stir with a stick will ensure rapid decomposition. Avoid defecating near streams and water bodies.

Wildlife Viewing: Spotting wildlife is always a thrill. A few tips:
- The best times for viewing are the "magic hours" of dusk and dawn.
- Look for signs of recent animal activity like tracks, scat, and recent feeding areas.
- When cresting a ridge or entering into a valley, scan the terrain for animal activity.
- Move slowly and quietly (except in heavy bear habitats) and travel downwind.
- Photographing wildlife requires skill, patience and (usually) some very specialized gear such as telephoto lenses. Use a fast film and have your camera ready for action.

Safety and Respect: It is illegal to feed or harass wildlife; fines can be very stiff. Besides, watching unaware animals conduct their lives from afar is more pleasurable than crowding a frightened or agitated beast. Stressed animals have lower survival rates and may become unpredictable. Besides, there's plenty of room for everyone.
Many animals in the Yukon are truly wild. You may be the first human they have ever seen! Be bear aware always, and bull moose aware during the fall rut. Remember, any animal may react if it feels threatened, especially a mother with young.

Hunting and Fishing: Many Yukoners provide for their families through hunting, trapping and fishing. Visitors are asked to respect these activities and to acquire appropriate licences if hunting or fishing. There are excellent fishing opportunities throughout the Yukon. A licence is required for locals and visitors; check out The Fish; page 20. Anglers should be aware of a few concerns. Even up in the remote north, some areas have been fished out. Consider traveling far off the beaten trail. Also, the use of barb-less hooks, non-lead sinkers, and using the "catch-and-release" method are highly recommended.

Dogs: A dog can be useful for packing as well as for invaluable companionship. On the flip side, most dogs will chase wildlife. Keep your dog restrained or leave it at home.
Dogs must be kept on a leash in parks like Kluane and the Chilkoot Pass. There is also controversy over dog and bear interaction. Some claim a dog will antagonize a bear, while others see dogs as a useful deterrent and early warning system. Its hard to say decisively which view holds more truth. If Rover comes with you, please respect other travelers as well as the wildlife.

BEARS

Travel: Bears are found throughout the territory; be bear aware everywhere. Travel in large parties (3-6) in heavy bear country and make yourself known. Yelling, singing, clapping and talking can be very effective in announcing your presence. This can be very important in areas where sight or sound are obscured, like windy ridges, dense forest, narrow canyons and rushing creeks. Whistling and small bells are questionable in their effectiveness.

Be aware of your surroundings. Look for fresh bear scat (droppings), paw prints, disturbed ground and fresh claw marks on trees. Leave an area immediately if you smell or see carrion (an animal corpse).

Consider traveling midday, especially when it's hot. Most bears nap during hot days. Never approach or feed a bear, especially a sow (Mama bear) with cubs. **NOTE:** All information in this guide is best supplemented with the excellent "Backcountry Basics" by Cave Smith, Greystone Books.

Camping: It is ESSENTIAL that bears do not associate food with humans. A bear hooked on people food is a dead bear, and it may take a few humans out on its tragic downward spiral.

Bears see with their noses; be aware of reducing odours around camp. Avoid smelly foods like bacon and sardines. Cook downwind and far away from your tent.

Cosmetics and toothpaste have been known to attract the omnivorous bear. Store anything odorous in a bear canister (bear proof, solid-plastic container) or in a pack hung 12 feet or more up in a tree and far from the trunk. In lieu of a tree, hang the pack over a steep cliff or, if no other options exist, put it under a big pile of rocks.

Women will need to be careful with proper disposal of feminine hygiene products. Consider burning them in a hot fire or wrapping carefully and packing out.

Encounters: Every bear encounter is different and no hard rules apply. Although it it's easier to say than do… KEEP CALM! Talk in a calm but firm voice to the bear. Move your hands slowly above your head to help the bear identify you better. Avoid strong eye contact and sudden movements. DON'T SCREAM OR RUN. Don't drop your pack as it may protect you if the bear attacks. In most cases simply stand your ground. A bear standing upright may be trying to smell you better. Many charges are broken off at the last second. Playing dead is generally only recommended if a grizzly attacks and makes contact In most cases fight off black bears (except sows with cubs) with anything possible. If attacked, lie on your stomach and keep still. Cover your head with your hands and use your pack to protect you.

Bear Deterrents: Reports have shown that cans of pepper spray can be an effective bear deterrent IF USED CORRECTLY. Do not dispense into the wind and make sure it is quickly and easily accessible.

NOTE: Before boarding any aircraft inform the pilot or crew that you have bear spray, and they will likely let you carry it in a sealed bag or other container.

The big bang and fireball of a pencil flare can be very effective in frightening a bear away. Proper dispensing of the flare is essential. If, for instance, you shoot the flare behind the bear it may run right at you! Bears hate noise! Banging pots and pans and other loud, shrill noises have been known to drive bears out of camp.

Guns are an extreme form of bear control but do have their time and place. It is illegal to carry firearms in Kluane National Park. You will require a license to carry a gun in the bush. Remember that prevention is always the best rule of thumb.

Black bear
Males: Average 250 pounds
Females: Average 175 pounds
Height: Up to 3 feet at shoulder
Lifespan: Up to 20+ years
Distinguishing Characteristics:
Straight nose, no hump, black to
blonde fur, shorter claws
Other Info: Excellent runner, swim-
mer and climber

Grizzly bear
Males: Average 400 pounds
Females: Average 250 pounds
Height: Up to 3 feet at shoulder
Lifespan: Up to 25+ years
Distinguishing Characteristics:
Concave nose, humped back, longer
claws, cinnamon to brown colour
Other Info: Excellent runner, swim-
mer, poor climber

NOTE: Be bear-aware and use common sense, but don't let fear ruin an otherwise enjoyable outing. After thousands of kilometres of back country travel I have seen very few bears in the bush. Of the ones I've seen, I've never had anything close to a dangerous encounter.

ADVANCED TRAVEL TIPS

Creek Crossings: Creeks can pose a considerable hazard if water levels are flowing high. Early mornings are the best crossing times. Look for a wide braided (divided) area; this may entail scouting up or, usually, downstream. Beware of deep and fast moving sections.

It's best to wear sandals, neoprene booties or old running shoes to cross; bare feet is considerably dangerous. Use a long stick, or better yet, a ski pole and keep a minimum of two points in contact with the creek bottom at all times.

Undo pack straps and cross facing upstream. The water is almost always icy cold; try to cross efficiently. Rocks and other objects may be obscured by silty waters.

Rocky Slopes: Exposed rock is usually defined as scree (smaller than fist size) and talus (larger than fist size). Wear appropriate footwear when climbing on rocky slopes; bigger boots are generally better. Scrambling fans will have lots of areas to play but should be aware of the crumbly nature of most Yukon rock. Try to anticipate loose, shifting rock. Get into the rhythm and get in touch with your inner mountain goat. The lichen on some rocks can be very slick if wet. One final tip: Try not to send rock tumbling onto your traveling companions.

Buckbrush: This brush usually consists of dense shrubs like willow, dwarf birch and alder. It often looks like good walking from a distance, but don't be fooled. Although this terrain is sometimes unavoidable, try to keep traveling through it to a minimum.

Late Snow: Late snow travel can be efficient and enjoyable by 'kick stepping' up and 'boot skiing' down. Be aware, however, of icy and inconsistent snow as well as what's at the bottom of the slope (run-out). Ice axes can make snow travel safer and more enjoyable. Knowing how to properly self-arrest (catching your fall with an ice axe) is critical.

Late snow is often slick and more stable in the mornings, softer and wetter by afternoon. Watch for areas that may be snow-loaded and primed for an avalanche, and avoid traveling on glaciers altogether.

Other Terrain: Canyons are sometimes encountered in mountainous areas and can't always be detected on a map. Remember to be flexible with your game plan. Tundra and grassy meadows often look inviting from a distance and can be a joy to travel over. Conversely, they can be wet and filled with tussocks (unstable protruding mats of grass and sedges) which would tax the patience of a saint.

(VERY) BASIC FIRST AID

Hypothermia: A rapid cooling of the body's core temperature.
Symptoms: Uncontrolled shivering followed by delirium and possible death.
Prevention: Stay warm, dry, fed, and rested. Monitor friends for symptoms.
Treatment: Get warm! Consume hot drinks, get shelter from wind and/or rain, add layers of clothing, make a good hot fire.

Blisters: Irritating skin rash caused by abrasion of skin.
Symptoms: Painful rash and/or bubbling of skin, usually on feet.
Prevention: Good foot care: double socks, dry feet, break in boots
Treatment: Apply moleskin or ductape upon the first feeling of burning sensation (hot spots). Air feet out, keep the painful area clean, reduce walking if possible.

Sunstroke: Prolonged exposure to hot, direct hot sun may lead to tissue damage, nausea etc.
Symptoms: Disorientation, nausea and vomiting, and possibly collapse.
Prevention: Beware of the hottest part of the day: 11 am - 3 pm. Keep hydrated and cover your head and body, use sunscreen nd sunglasses.
Treatment: Seek shade, rest and water.

Insect Stings: Bees, hornets and wasps may sting if they feel threatened.
Symptoms: Sharp pain, possible allergic reaction.
Prevention: Be aware of habitat; bring sting medication; know the allergies of travel mates.
Treatment: First: do not remove the stinger by squeezing it. Use a pin or knife edge on the skin to scrape off the stinger. If the reaction is severe, use medication; apply something cool to reduce the swelling.

Sprained Ankle: Sudden painful strain of ankle ligaments.
Symptoms: Varying difficulties in walking.
Prevention: Wear good solid footwear with strong ankle support; pay attention to terrain, especially loose rock and slick surfaces.
Treatment: Rest if possible, bind something tight around the ankle, improvise a crutch, use travelling partners for assistance in walking.

SUMMER SPORTS

Swimming: Although much of the water in the Territory rarely warms up, small lakes can be refreshing on hot days. Many communities also operate outdoor pools during the summer. See page 167.

Lucky Lake, which operates a water slide on hot days, and Watson Lake (page 54) can both be excellent for swimming.

Whitehorse has a number of lakes worthy of a dip. Local favorites include Long Lake (page 60) and Ear Lake (page 62). Pine Lake (page 110) near Haines Junction has a nice beach and a floating dock. Also consider Coal Lake (page 130) near Carmacks, and some of the 'tailing ponds' (water-filled mining pits) around Dawson. Be cautious with this last option; if plants grow in the pond it is probably fine.

Soaking: There is only one developed hot spring in the Yukon, and two just outside of the Territory.

• The Takhini Hot Springs are found about 29 km from the Whitehorse city centre and are open year-round. To get to the springs follow the Alaska Highway west out of Whitehorse and turn right onto the Klondike Highway, about 13 km from downtown. Follow this road for 6 km and turn left at a obviously marked road junction. Follow the Takini Hot Springs Road for 10 km.

The springs are fairly commercialized, offering change rooms, a sauna, and a restaurant for a $4.50 entrance fee.

• The Atlin Warm Springs offer a mellow soak in warm, not hot, water. Check out Hike # 03, page 58. Continue for another 18 km past the Mount Monarch trail head (a total of 23 km along the Warm Bay road). The undeveloped springs are on your left with a primitive camping area nearby.

• The Liard Hot Springs, found 265 km south of Watson Lake (km 765), are a perfect example of semi-developed hot springs. They are free of charge and open year round. This is a must-stop if traveling on the Alaska Highway.

Running: Many of the lower elevation trails and old roads in this book are excellent for jogging. Look for hikes with little elevation gains and stable surfaces (see 'Concerns' box). There are many good running trails in the Whitehorse area. Be sure to watch for local landmarks so as not to get lost and be bear aware especially if you are in Kluane National Park.

Runners may also be interested in summer races like the Midnight Dome race in Dawson and the Skagway to Whitehorse Relay. Contact Sports Yukon, page 175, for more information.

Mountain Biking: There are some excellent single-track (foot traffic/ biking) trails in the Whitehorse area as well as many old roads near the smaller communities. Check in the "Merits" box found before each hike.

NOTE: Mountain bikers need to be people and bear-aware while in the bush. Make lots of noise. A repair kit is recommended especially in more remote areas. Please stay on the trails whenever possible, to preserve the integrity of your surroundings, and don't forget the essentials like ample food and water, helmets, etc.

The Whitehorse area (Hikes 4-7) as well as the Skagway area (Hike 14; Options 2 and 3) have some great single-track biking. Trails can be muddy and wet in the springtime. Much of the terrain is challenging with some "technical" (advanced) sections.

For old roads consider Cantlie Lake (Hike 6, Option 2), the Ibex Valley (Hike 8), Mush Lake (Hike 21, Option 1), the Alsek Road (Hike 24, Option 3) and the Ridge Road Heritage Trail near Dawson (Hike 36). Some muddy and steep sections may be encountered.

Bike Touring: The scenery is fantastic but the roads are long, occasionally rough, with few communities and services in between. Consider the following tips:
- Headwinds generally come in from the north (Arctic) or the south (Pacific systems) with the latter dominating.
- Road construction is a common occurrence during the brief Yukon summer.
- Boil or treat (filter, add iodine pills) roadside water for safety.

See Chapter 6 for campgrounds, highway information and a weather report phone number. Contact Sports Yukon (page 175) for race information.

Paddling in the Yukon: Yukon waterways are wild, beautiful and full of history, but are potentially very dangerous. Great care must be taken in planning and preparation, especially on longer and remote trips. It is common for people to exceed their limits so please resist the temptation to do so. For well-prepared parties the Yukon offers some of the best paddling in the world.

Timing is everything on northern rivers; a water level too low or too high could present formidable difficulties. Rivers usually break in May. The highest flow is normally in June with the exception of glacier-fed rivers which are more dynamic and variable.

Small lakes can be enjoyable for canoe outings, but the larger lakes are best reserved for sea kayaks. Sea kayaking is particularly good on Atlin Lake and around Haines, Alaska. Also consider the Southern Lakes region (Nares, Bennett, Marsh and Tagish.). Be very aware of strong winds on larger lakes. If in doubt, cross early in the morning. Regardless of the type of boat used, always wear a life jacket, travel in a group, and be respectful of the icy waters.

Day Trips can be had on portions of the Yukon River. Slightly more advanced river trips include the Klondike near Dawson, the Dezedeash near Haines Junction, and the Takhini west of Whitehorse.

Experienced whitewater paddlers may wish to consider day trips on the Tatshenshini, Lapie and Blanchard rivers.

Extended Trips: The mighty Yukon River is by far the most popular river trip in the Territory. Due to its fascinating history and a relatively easy level of difficulty, the river continues to draw thousands of people annually. Most parties float from Whitehorse or Carmacks to Dawson, a trip of one to two weeks. Moderate one to two week trips can be made on the Big Salmon or Teslin rivers, both tributaries of the Yukon River. Also consider the Nisutlin river near Teslin. For whitewater fans, the rivers that drain into the Peel (Bonnett Plume, Snake and Wind) offer lengthy trips with up to Class III water. All require a fly-in.

The Tatshenshini/Alsek River system, now protected by BC Parks and Kluane National Park, offers remote wilderness, glaciers, and no small amount of rain. The Nahanni River, to the east of the Yukon, has massive canyons, hot springs, and the epic Virginia Falls (which is twice the height of Niagara Falls). Contact BC Parks (page 172) for the Tashenshini and Nahanni National Park, Postal Bag 300, Fort Simpson, NWT X0E 0N0 for the Nahanni River.

Climbing (Top-Rope): **NOTE:** Rock climbing, even bouldering, should not be attempted without a thorough knowledge of climbing techniques and equipment. For more information on climbing in the Yukon check recommended reading (page 176) or contact the Yukon Climbing Association via Sports Yukon (page 175). The club holds special events, and operates an indoor climbing wall in the off-season.

Top-rope climbers may be interested in the following three areas which have some clean routes:

• **The Rock Gardens** have about 30 clean and semi-clean routes of about 30 to 40 feet in height. They are found by traveling out of Whitehorse on South Access Road (a.k.a. Robert Service Way) to the Alaska Highway. Take a left and follow for less than ½ km. Turn right onto Lobird (a.k.a. Maclean) Road and follow it to the first right, a small, rough road. Park here or continue to a parking area that dips down to your right, about 1/4 km in. Pick up foot trails in the forest near the end of the parking area and follow to the bluffs. The clean routes are mainly found near a fenced in pond. Climbs rate from 5.6 to 5.11 and six or seven have top bolts.

NOTE: Don't leave valuables in vehicles as the place is periodically visited by thieving varmints.

• **Crocus Bluffs** can be located by following the Klondike Highway to just outside Dawson. See page 142. There are about 4 or 5 semi-clean routes and some chains found at the top of the 40-foot pitch. Be cautious of loose rock and wear a helmet. Climbs are 5.5 to 5.7 with a few harder moves possible.

• **Golden Canyons** has some of the best intermediate and advanced climbing in the Territory. Follow directions for the Takini Hot Springs, page 44. Turn left just before the springs onto the Takini River Road. Follow this rough road for 13 km. (One section 11 km in may be impassable; park here and walk the rest.) A foot path to the canyons can be found on the right side of the road near a small pond.

Climbs rated 5.7 to 5.12 can be found in the canyons, mainly on the right side. Look for top bolts and practice extreme caution when setting up ropes above the climbs.

Advanced Climbing: Unfortunately, no clean multi-pitch routes exist in the Yukon. There is some good ice in the territory, but the access is often lengthy. Mountaineers must contact Parks Canada (page 172) if planning a trip to one of the Kluane giants. Mount Logan is a perennial favourite with most parties taking the Kings Trench, a moderate but unstable route up an icy passage to the Logan plateau. Not for amateurs.

WINTER SPORTS

The Yukon can be a winter wonderland, particularly from February to April. Nice sunny days and clear, moonlit nights are common.
The Yukon, as everyone knows, can get very cold. Learn to recognize the first signs of hypothermia and remember the layering system: add when cold, shed when hot. Pack hot food and liquids like soups and tea. Winter travel can be slow, so budget ample time. In several locations avalanches can occur; check with knowledgeable local people before you enter these areas and be prepared with the proper gear.

Cross Country Skiing: Yukoners love to ski! It's undeniably one of the best ways to beat the winter blues. Many small communities like Haines Junction, Watson Lake, Dawson, and Carcross have semi-maintained ski trails. Whitehorse excels for track set trails with about 70 km of groomed trail systems found at the Mount McIntyre Ski centre (phone 668-4477). Chadburn Lake (page 66) has more than 20 km of locally set and marked trails.
For those who like to ski on snowmobile trails the list is endless. Many of the hikes on old roads in this guide are snowmobile trails in the winter.
NOTE: Keep your eyes, ears and nostrils open for these fast-moving machines.
Numerous skiing races occur in the Whitehorse area throughout the winter. Biathlon fans may wish to check out the range up on the Grey Mountain Road near Whitehorse. Contact these clubs through Sports Yukon, page175.

Back-country Skiing, Snowshoeing: In general, the sugary snow of the Territory is tough to break trail in. However, wind-swept areas like the Chilkat (Haines) Pass and the White Pass can be excellent as long as one is avalanche-aware. A good base is usually established by March.
Frozen rivers can provide efficient access in good conditions. Also, consider some of the hikes in this guide.

Ski-joring and Dogmushing: The use of dogs for transportation has a long history in the North, starting with the native peoples, into the gold rush era, and on to the international races and hobby mushers of today. Ski-joring, a toned-down method of dog mushing, originated in Sweden and is growing in popularity throughout the north. A "ski-jorer" places up to three dogs in racing harnesses and attaches them with a shock absorbing and quick-release line to said skier. A truly adventurous way to experience the joys of winter!

Those with a yearning to mush a team of spirited dogs over frozen field and forest should contact local mushers. Trips can be custom-made for all ages and interests. Quick outings and multi-day trips are all available.

The 'Yukon Quest' is a great way to see dog drivers in action. This 1600 km endurance contest runs from Whitehorse through Dawson and on to Fairbanks, Alaska. This annual event has been taking place for over twenty years. Atlin, Haines Junction, and Dawson also have a number of exciting dog races.

NOTE: Skiers and ski-jorers may wish to challenge sections of these trails after the dogs have gone, as they can be in excellent condition.

Alpine Fun: There are two ski hills in the Yukon. Both are smaller scale hills, but can provide a good challenge for most people. Mount Sima (1100 feet drop) in Whitehorse has ten runs of varying difficulty. The Watson Lake ski hill has a 500 foot drop. Although it is a small hill, it can be good fun for beginners and intermediates.

Telemark skiers and back country snowboarders may wish to check out either the White or Chilkat (Haines) Passes. Conditions can be superb in the spring season. Be very cautious of avalanches and whiteout conditions. Log Cabin (page 85) and Mount Montana (page 78) are also local favorites. In addition, the nearby town of Atlin, BC, offers some of the finest heli-skiing in the world.

Ed Vos

The author skijoring with his dogs

ADVANCED HIKES

The following hikes are extended back-country trips requiring a lot of planning. They were not included in the following chapters due to their over-specialized appeal. Hopefully, this information can get you started.

Trans-Canada Trail: The Yukon section of this lengthy trail can be used by hikers, bikers, horseback riders, skiers and snowmobilers. At the time of writing the only completed sections were around Whitehorse and up to Braeburn Lodge, which is a fun multi-day ski trip, as well as a good back-country bike tour. Due to tight budgets and sheer geography much of the trail is slated to follow highways like the Dempster. For more information contact the Klondike Snowmobile Association at P.O. Box 9034, 24 Wann Road, Whitehorse, Yukon Y1A 4A4.
Website: www.ksa.yk.ca

North Canol Heritage Trail: This 355 km section of the historic Canol Road can be done in sections, or in its entirety, and is known as one of the toughest hikes in Canada. One trailhead is found at the Macmillan Pass northeast of Ross River; the road is usually somewhat drivable. The other trailhead is found across the Mackenzie River from Norman Wells in the Northwest Territories.
This trip entails at least one fly-in, several river crossings, and the dangers of being very remote. Food caches are another must if doing the entire trail. While some sections of the road are easy walking, much of the road is rapidly being reclaimed by nature. Nonetheless, the trail may appeal to those wanting a very challenging wilderness experience. For more information contact: Sahtu Tourism Association: P.O. Box 115, Norman Wells, Northwest Territories, Canada X0E (867) 587-2054.

The Pipeline Fire Road to Tombstone Range: This hike, which follows a rough road for 50 km and a difficult bushwhack to the Tombstone Range, looks like a fine challenge and may be included in the next printing of this guide. It could take up to a week to hike, covers over 90 km and requires a keen eye for routes as well as good map reading skills. Since it doesn't make a full loop, a vehicle should be waiting at the far trailhead. For a brief overview check out "Along the Dempster" by Walter Lanz; page 000.

Donjek Glacier Loop: This trail was excluded due to the difficulty and length of the hike (see page 126). This 88 km route travels through stunning wilderness and may appeal to 'hardcore' hiking enthusiasts. A fly-in is another possible option. Contact Parks Canada (page 172) for more information.

CHAPTER 3

WHITEHORSE REGION

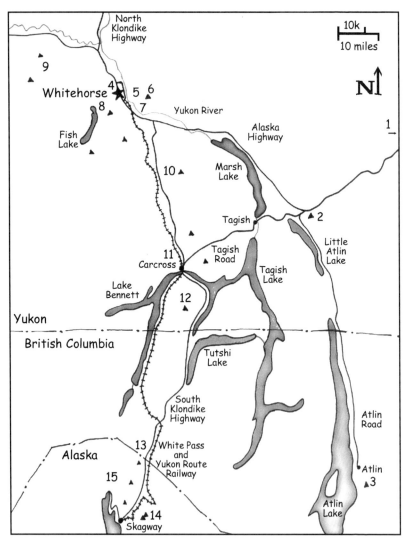

1 Watson Lake Walks	6. Grey Mountain	11. Carcross Desert
2 Mount White	7. Whitehorse Lakes	12. Mount Montana
3. Monarch Mountain	8. Ibex Valley	13. Feather Peak
4. Whitehorse Walks	9. Fish Lake Area	14. Dewey Lakes
5. Miles Canyon	10. Mount Lorne	15. Chilkoot Pass

The Area: The Whitehorse Area, as described in this guide, extends from Watson Lake to Whitehorse and then down the South Klondike Highway to Skagway, Alaska. This is the land of the Kaska and the Tlingit, the Tagish and the Tutchone. Naturalists will surely enjoy the great variety of flora and fauna in this broad region while history buffs will find the Klondike goldrush and Yukon First Nations' history of interest.

Watson Lake is known as "the Gateway to the Yukon," and has a number of popular visitor attractions like the Signpost Forest and the Northern Lights Centre.

About two-thirds of Yukoners live in Whitehorse, the Territories capital. The city is situated in an enormous valley which is marked by clay cliffs and former lake fronts, and serves as the supply depot of the Territory.

Traveling southward the mountains get larger as the picturesque town of Carcross and its miniature 'desert' is found. Continuing along the South Klondike Highway the spectacular White Pass is reached. On clear days glaciers can be seen all around, and this is a great place to look for alpine flowers when in season.

After the summit of the Pass it's a long, steep descent into the mountains and lush forestscapes of the Pacific Coast. Skagway, a bustling tourist town, is worth a quick visit, but the true magic lies in the mountains and forests of the area.

Walks and Hikes: The Chilkoot Pass is the most famous trail in the region. It is an excellent and challenging trail with many historical remains and diverse eco-systems. However, such a trip demands considerable preparation.

A number of shorter hikes in the Skagway area are great for exploring the lush coastal rainforests. The White Pass area, north of Skagway, has a short and rainy season for hiking, but on a nice day it's hard to beat. Glacier lovers are sure to be satisfied as well as off-trail enthusiasts.

Carcross offers easy strolls along the beachfront or in what is known as the world's smallest desert. Fans of scrambling may wish to check out Mount Lorne, found on the way to Whitehorse.

Whitehorse, the wilderness city, has an amazing number of trails, both single-track and old roads, within the town limits. Most are great for hiking, biking, and skiing. Some excellent opportunities for advanced hiking and scrambling can be found in the mountains around the outskirts of Whitehorse. Finally, Watson Lake has a number of short, interpreted walks as well as several nice lakes in which to swim.

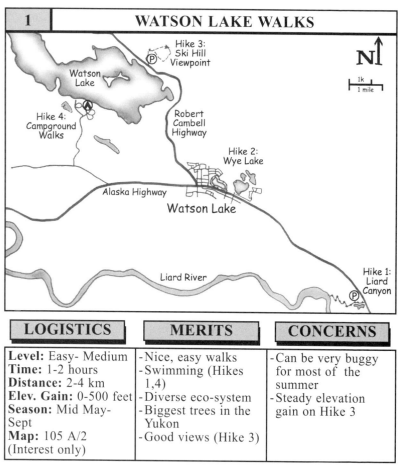

LOGISTICS	MERITS	CONCERNS
Level: Easy- Medium **Time:** 1-2 hours **Distance:** 2-4 km **Elev. Gain:** 0-500 feet **Season:** Mid May-Sept **Map:** 105 A/2 (Interest only)	-Nice, easy walks -Swimming (Hikes 1,4) -Diverse eco-system -Biggest trees in the Yukon -Good views (Hike 3)	-Can be very buggy for most of the summer -Steady elevation gain on Hike 3

Hike 1: Lucky Lake/Liard Canyon.   Easy. 4 km and 1-2 hours return.

The Lucky Lake Recreation area is found 9 km southeast of the center of Watson Lake on the Alaska Highway (km 1012). A swim at the lake after a hot and dusty day on the highway is highly recommended. The marked trailhead and parking area is found on your right next to a cemetery.

From the parking area walk towards the lake. Look for a trailhead/map found by the fence near the parking area. Follow hiking signs along the side of the lake.

Continue on this old road, past some outhouses, as it meanders slowly down to a viewing station of the Liard River canyon and rapids. Consider dropping down to the waterfront from here. Head right and follow the shoreline to a white sand beach several hundred metres away. This is a good place to look for interesting plants and rocks. On a hot day it is a real pleasure to wander about barefoot.

Hike 2: Wye Lake. Easy. 2 km. Up to 1 hour loop.

Wye Lake is found in the center of town. The trail can be accessed from many different locations. Follow the Alaska Highway into Watson Lake. Look for a road (8th Street north) across the road from the Northern Lights Building. Follow 8th Street 2 blocks up to the park on your right. The gazebo is a good starting point.

This easy loop is a great leg-stretcher and introduction to Yukon flora and fauna. The home-made interpretive signs are well put together and illustrate the local native peoples' connection with the plant world. The trails are occasionally braided with a number of small spur trails; simply stay on the main trail nearest the lake.

Hike 3: Ski Hill Viewpoint. Medium. 2.5 km. 2 hour loop.

NOTE: This trail is good for those wishing a little workout rewarded by views of Watson Lake (the lake, not the town) and the distant Cassiar and Pelly mountain ranges. It involves a steep elevation gain of about 500 feet and there may be late snow encountered early in the season.

From Watson Lake get onto the Robert Campbell Highway. Follow it for 7 km. Look for signs marking the ski hill road, which is found on your right. Follow this road up to a gate. A sign says there is no turnaround; in fact, there is ample room for parking and turning around near the gate. Follow the road up by foot to the chalet which is less than 0.5 km walk. A steep road in front of the chalet follows to the left of the chairlift. Look for raspberries and strawberries if in season.

Follow it up for about 20 minutes to a good lookout of the area. Turn around here or, better yet, stay on the road as it loops downward for a more moderate descent through wildflowers back to the chalet.

Hike 4: Watson Lake Campground Trails. Easy. 2 km and up to 1 hour return.

This 1 km-long trail hooks up the lower and upper campground loops. The top end of the trail is located between campsites # 7 and # 8. Follow it through the forest to campsites # 38 and # 36. Continue walking in the same direction to reach Watson Lake which can be good for swimming. Return by the same route, or if starting at the bottom campground loop, hike to the upper loop. A .5 km return trail with good views of the lake can be found between campsites # 14 and # 15.

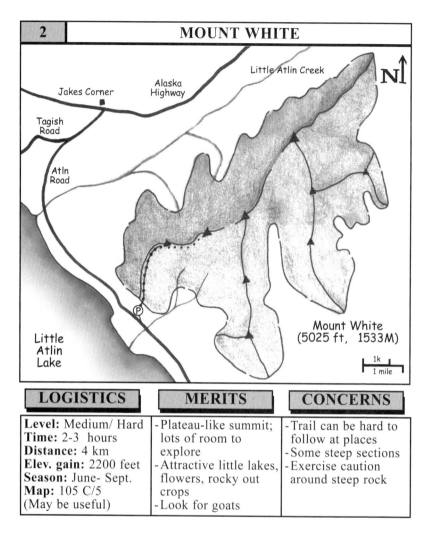

LOGISTICS	MERITS	CONCERNS
Level: Medium/ Hard **Time:** 2-3 hours **Distance:** 4 km **Elev. gain:** 2200 feet **Season:** June- Sept. **Map:** 105 C/5 (May be useful)	-Plateau-like summit; lots of room to explore -Attractive little lakes, flowers, rocky out crops -Look for goats	-Trail can be hard to follow at places -Some steep sections -Exercise caution around steep rock

From Whitehorse drive east on the Alaska Highway for 78 km to Jakes Corner (km 1392). Turn right onto the Atlin/Tagish Road. Turn left 2 km from here onto the Atlin Road. Follow it for about 6.5 km. A little gravel road found on the left side of the Atlin Road cuts sharply in the opposite direction in which you are traveling. Follow it up for about 50 metres until it ends at a noisy, orange generator. Park here.

The trail can be picked up behind the generator; drop down and cross the creek. From here the path will begin to head up, becoming quite vague in sections. Look for clues like old cables and other bric-a-brac. The forest thins out just a short way up with excellent views of Little

Atlin Lake emerging. Keep track of where the trail fades away as it may be hard to spot on the way down; the trail/route generally follows the shoulder of the ridge. A transmitter tower about 2 km up is a possible turn-around, or else consider the following option:

Option: Mount White Plateau. Medium. Add up to 12 km. 1-6 hours return.
For those with time and energy, this high ground has unlimited potential for exploration. By continuing along the ridge the plateau area can be reached. Little lakes and rocky outcrops abound. It is possible to reach the true summit of Mount White by continuing in a northeast direction; this would take a full day. Some route-finding skills will be necessary to pick your way through a forested area. Have fun!

Operation "Billy Drop": In 1983-1984 the Yukon Department of Renewable Resources flew in a number of mountain goats to Mount White. At present it appears to have been a successful endeavour as sightings of this unique animal are fairly common in this area.

Facts about mountain goats:
• Their closest relatives are antelopes, not sheep or goats.
• Males are called 'billies' and females 'nannies'.
• Nannies also have horns and give birth to 1 or 2 kids in the spring.
• Although the nannies are a little smaller in size, they rule the roost.
• Mountain goats have specialized hooves which enable them to scale cliffs that would intimidate some rock climbers.
• They are very poor runners but can leap up to 12 feet!

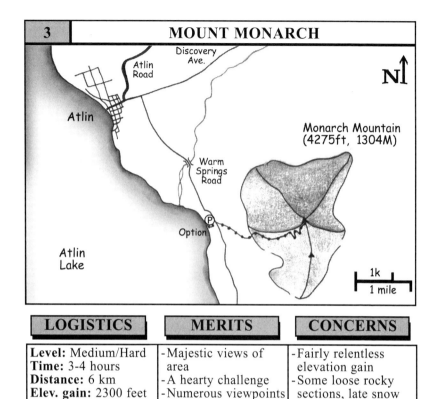

LOGISTICS	MERITS	CONCERNS
Level: Medium/Hard **Time:** 3-4 hours **Distance:** 6 km **Elev. gain:** 2300 feet **Season:** June - Sept. **Map:** 104 N/12 (Interest only)	- Majestic views of area - A hearty challenge - Numerous viewpoints en route	- Fairly relentless elevation gain - Some loose rocky sections, late snow - Brushy on top

From the town of Atlin, BC, follow Discovery Avenue out of town. After a little over 0.5km, turn right onto Warm Bay Road. Follow it for about 5.5 km. You will pass the Atlin Art Centre on your left, and just past it look for a parking area on your right. The Mount Monarch trailhead is marked as well as a trailhead for a path that leads down to a beach (Option 1).

Follow the foot trail across the road until it hits a public road. The trail can be a little hard to pick up from here. Turn right at the road and walk for approximately 20 metres to where the trail begins again. Look for rock cairns and signposts to guide you.

After this section the trail continues to steadily gain elevation. Numerous viewing stations en route to the summit provide opportunities to rest the haunches and re-hydrate. The trail braids a little near the top; stay on the main path that lead to your right. This mountain has no distinct summit, but a viewing station at the end of the trail is marked by rock cairns. There are some exploration options up top, but generally the rocky terrain and dense foliage is not too inviting. Return by the same route.

Option: Atlin Beach. Easy. .25 km and .5 hour return.

From the parking area, simply follow a short, maintained trail down to a pleasant section of beachfront. Very nice on hot sunny days.
NOTE: The Atlin area has many old roads for hiking and biking. A look at the map 104/ N (1:250,000) can be helpful for planning a trip.

View Explained: From the summit of Monarch Mountain, the following features are visible on a clear day:
Looking south down Atlin Lake, a portion of the massive Llewellyn Glacier can be spotted which is part of the simply enormous Juneau Ice Cap. The Llewellyn glacier is found in Atlin Provincial Park, British Columbia's third-largest park. Atlin Lake, which dominates the views to the west, is over 140 km long and is the largest natural lake in BC. It is increasingly popular with sea kayakers and anglers.
Teresa Island can be seen about 8 km away to the southwest. Birch Mountain, found on Teresa Island, is the highest point of land in a fresh water lake in the world. To the north of it, Atlin Mountain has an excellent example of a rock glacier. Rock glaciers are formed when glaciers get covered with rocky debris. Finally, the historic town of Atlin is obvious to the northwest. Several interesting books have been written about Atlin's goldrush, and are well worth checking out.

Jean Cambell Collection

The sternwheeler Tarahne docked in Atlin.

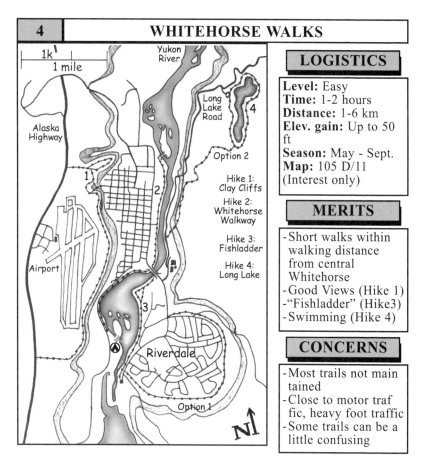

LOGISTICS

Level: Easy
Time: 1-2 hours
Distance: 1-6 km
Elev. gain: Up to 50 ft
Season: May - Sept.
Map: 105 D/11 (Interest only)

MERITS

- Short walks within walking distance from central Whitehorse
- Good Views (Hike 1)
- "Fishladder" (Hike 3)
- Swimming (Hike 4)

CONCERNS

- Most trails not maintained
- Close to motor traffic, heavy foot traffic
- Some trails can be a little confusing

Hike 1: Clay Cliffs.   Easy. Up to 4 km and 1 hour return.

Follow Black Street in Whitehorse away from the river to a ravine marked by a fence and gate. A trail to the left of the gulch leads steeply up to a 'bench' (raised flatland) overlooking town and the Whitehorse airport. By going to the right the trail leads to a viewpoint of the area. By following the trail to the left, it goes along the airport fence with good views of the city. Return by the same way or loop back to town by following one of several steep trails that lead down to the railroad tracks. The next hike can be added to this one to make a loop.

Hike 2: Whitehorse Walkway.   Easy. Up to 6 km and 2 hours return.

This trails connects Kishwoot Island in Whitehorse with the Robert Service Campground. Pick it up at any point for a relaxing stroll.

From Kishwoot Island follow the trail/sidewalk between the railroad tracks and the water. Look for historical relics and interpretive displays. The trail passes through Rotary Park, under the Yukon River bridge and eventually to the Robert Service Campground. The paved trail ends near the Robert Service campground, which has a short foot trail to a small island in the Yukon River. Return by the same route or follow the railroad tracks across the road back to town.

Hike 3: Whitehorse Fishladder.   Easy. 4 km and 1-2 hours return.

From downtown Whitehorse go down to the Yukon River and pick up the foot trail (previous hike). Take a right on it and walk to the Yukon River bridge. Proceed underneath the bridge and then over it. Pick up an unofficial trail that parallels the Yukon River that is found immediately to your right. This trail has numerous braided sections. Simply stay between the river and the road. Follow it for 2 km to the Fish Ladder and Whitehorse Dam.

Option 1: Riverdale Loop.   Easy. Add 2 km and up to 1 hour.

This trail can be picked up near the Fish Ladder and can be used to turn Hike 3 into a loop. Look for a wide trail to the left of the Chadburn Lake Road. The trail parallels the road and circles around Riverdale eventually rejoining Second Avenue within view of the Yukon River bridge.

Hike 4: Long Lake.   Easy. 1 km and up to 1 hour loop.

To reach Long Lake, cross the Yukon River Bridge and take the first left. Drive or bike towards the hospital and take a left onto Wickstrom Road (a.k.a.. Long Lake Road). Follow this road for 4 km to a parking area, on your right near the lake.
The walk around the lake is easy and straightforward, but do watch out for the many roots that tend to trip the unsuspecting walker. Stay on the path that parallels the banks of the lake. This is a good swimming hole on hot days.

Option 2: Hospital Loop.   Medium. Add 3 km and 1 hour.

It is possible to return to town via a system of foot trails. Pick up a trail at the south end of the lake, marked by a rest bench. Follow it to a trail junction and head right. Another junction is soon reached, head left and follow the trail that hugs the cliffs back to the hospital. If this trail is confusing, use local landmarks to guide you.

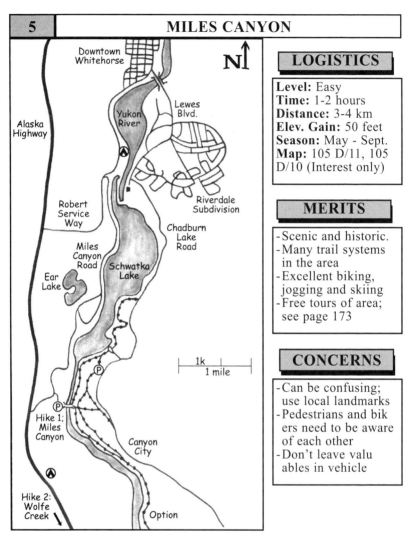

LOGISTICS

Level: Easy
Time: 1-2 hours
Distance: 3-4 km
Elev. Gain: 50 feet
Season: May - Sept.
Map: 105 D/11, 105 D/10 (Interest only)

MERITS

- Scenic and historic.
- Many trail systems in the area
- Excellent biking, jogging and skiing
- Free tours of area; see page 173

CONCERNS

- Can be confusing; use local landmarks
- Pedestrians and bikers need to be aware of each other
- Don't leave valuables in vehicle

There are a number of ways to get to Miles Canyon. Consider the following:

1) From downtown Whitehorse follow Robert Service Way (a.k.a. South Access Road) out of town for 1.5 km. Shortly after passing the Robert Service campground take a left onto the (marked) Miles Canyon Road. Follow for about 3 km and turn left onto the marked road towards the canyon. The parking area by the bridge is less than .5 km in.

2) From downtown Whitehorse follow Robert Service Way (a.k.a. South Access Road) to the Alaska Highway; about 2.5 km. Take a left here and follow the road for 3 km. Take another left at the top of the (marked)

Miles Canyon Road and follow this road down to the parking lot by the bridge.

3) This area is also accessible from the Chadburn Lake Road; page 66.

Cross the suspension bridge near the picnic area and follow one of two trails to Canyon City. The trail immediately to the right of the bridge follows an occasionally rocky footpath to the historic site. The next trail up on the right is an easier route. Not much remains of the former First Nations' camps and goldrush era dwellings. Return by either trail back to the bridge or consider continuing on via the option below or exploring the Chadburn Lake trail system (page 66-67).

Option: Yukon River. Medium. Add up to 4 hours and up to 12 km return to first hike.

Follow the first hike to Canyon City. From here a series of trails parallels the river upstream. Try to stay within eye and ear of the Yukon

T.R. Lane Collection

River. The trail is fairly easy to follow at first with some ups and downs. About four km upstream the trail veers away from the river and follows a former embankment. A good turnaround point is reached after a further 2 km of travel; adventurous souls may wish to follow this increasingly vague trail further.

Hike 2: Wolf Creek Campground. Easy. 3 km and 1 hour loop.

Drive up Robert Service Way (a.k.a. South Access Road) to the intersection with the Alaska Highway. Turn left and drive for 11 km. The campground is found on the left side of the highway. Park here or follow the campground loop to the marked trail head, under .5 km.

Look for interpretive pamphlets at the trailhead. Hike or bike the left branch of the trail to a viewpoint of the Yukon River about halfway in. Continue on the main trail to complete the loop.

Above is historic Miles Canyon, once a serious impediment to First Nations and gold seekers.

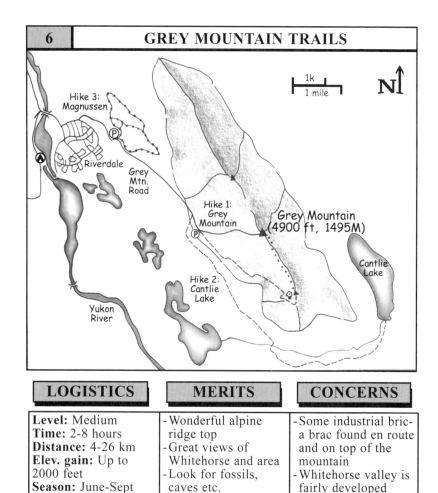

LOGISTICS	MERITS	CONCERNS
Level: Medium **Time:** 2-8 hours **Distance:** 4-26 km **Elev. gain:** Up to 2000 feet **Season:** June-Sept **Map:** 105 D/10 (May be useful)	- Wonderful alpine ridge top - Great views of Whitehorse and area - Look for fossils, caves etc. - Biking, skiing options	- Some industrial bric-a-brac found en route and on top of the mountain - Whitehorse valley is fairly developed

Hike 1: Grey Mountain. Medium. Up to 12 km and 4-5 hours return.

From downtown Whitehorse follow 2nd Avenue towards Riverdale. Cross the Yukon River bridge; the Sternwheeler "S.S. Klondike" will be to your right. Follow this road till you reach the first set of lights. Turn left here onto Alsek Boulevard. Take the second left onto Grey Mountain Road. Drive for 6.5 km to a large parking area on your right. From the parking area, simply follow the road up by foot. A transmitter tower will appear and disappear in the distance. The tower is a possible turnaround point; however, a trip to the summit ridge, now visible to the northwest, is well worth the effort. Vague foot-trails will take you up to where you belong: "... where the eagles fly, on mountains high..."

Hike 2: Cantlie Lake: Medium. 26 km and 5-7 hours return.

This old road is located 5.5 km up the Grey Mountain Road (see Hike 1), on the right side and almost directly across from the rifle range. The Grey Mountain parking and viewing area is a further 1 km up from here. A number of junctions will be encountered en route to the lake; simply stay left at every one. The trail can be choppy and muddy at places, and a number of large hills will be encountered on the way.
NOTE: I recommend biking this road although it is possible to reach the lake or return to the Grey Mountain Road via a very arduous bush-whack.

Hike 3: Magnussen. Medium. 4-9 km and 1-2 hours loop.

NOTE: This is a popular bike or ski trail near town although it is not as appealing for hiking.
The trail head is on your left about 2 km up the Grey Mountain Road (see Hike 1). Pass the cemetery and less than 1 km further look for the unmarked trailhead just past where the powerline crosses the road. There are usually cars parked here and a "no dogs allowed" sign is found in the woods to the right of the gravel pit.
Stay straight on the main trail at the start of the hike. The trail ascends and soon reaches a trail junction with a sign/map. This is a good place to customize your hike or bike. Stay to the left to reach a spur trail to a viewpoint. Turn around here for a short hike, continue along the main trail or do a partial loop.

View Explained: From the summit ridge of Grey Mountain there are excellent views of the Whitehorse area. Marsh Lake is the large lake to the southeast and the big mountain to the right of it is Mount Lorne, (Hike # 10). Far down the valley sits Mount Montana, (Hike # 12). Its often snow-covered glacier can be seen on clear days.
Nestled near the base of Grey Mountain one can spy numerous little lakes, (Hike # 07), as well as the Yukon River, (Hike # 05). Across the valley from here sits Golden Horn Mountain (Hike # 09), with the Mount Sima ski hill to the left of it.
Mount McIntyre, a long gentle ridge, sits to the northwest with Fish Lake tucked out of view behind it. Whitehorse is impossible to miss, and far to the west of it lies the Ibex Valley (Hike # 08), only partially visible. Finally, part of the enormous Lake Laberge, made famous by Robert Service, can be spotted almost due north.

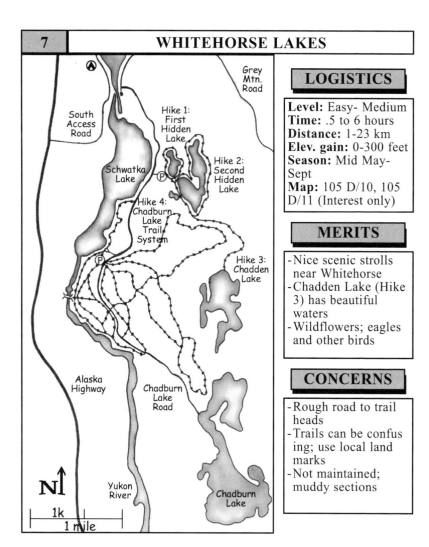

LOGISTICS

Level: Easy- Medium
Time: .5 to 6 hours
Distance: 1-23 km
Elev. gain: 0-300 feet
Season: Mid May-
Sept
Map: 105 D/10, 105
D/11 (Interest only)

MERITS

- Nice scenic strolls
  near Whitehorse
- Chadden Lake (Hike
  3) has beautiful
  waters
- Wildflowers; eagles
  and other birds

CONCERNS

- Rough road to trail
  heads
- Trails can be confus
  ing; use local land
  marks
- Not maintained;
  muddy sections

Hike 1: First Hidden Lake. Easy. 0.5 km and 0.5 hour loop.

From Whitehorse walk or bike across the Yukon River bridge. Take a
right onto Nisutlin Drive, which is the next intersection after the lights.
Follow it to just before the Whitehorse Dam. Turn left onto the Chadden
Lake Road which starts with a large elevation gain. Drive for 2 km.
Look for a rough but drivable road to your left. Follow this pot-holed
road for 0.3 km to a cul-de-sac. Park here.

Look for a trail to the left that goes slightly above the lake. This braided and sometimes confusing trail is best followed by always trying to
keep the lake to your right.

Hike 2: Second Hidden Lake. Medium. 3 km and an up to 1.5 hour loop.

Follow the driving instructions for the previous hike. Pick up an ATV (all terrain vehicle) trail to the right of the parking area. Follow it until the second lake comes into view. Walk along a sometimes confusing series of trails that follow the perimeter of the lake. This hike is easiest if you follow more established trails and always keep the lake to your left.

Hike 3: Chadden Lake. Medium. 5 km and 2-3 hours return.

Follow the driving instructions for Hike 1. From the cul-de-sac pick up a trail to the right of the first lake that initially goes to Second Hidden Lake. Stay on the main trail and turn right at every major trail junction. The trail goes through some steep sections, bypasses a few ponds, then reaches a marked split in the trail some 2 km from the trailhead.

Follow the left trail to reach an excellent viewpoint of the emerald-coloured waters of Chadden Lake. Turn around here, drop down to the lake or consider trekking further along the left (east) side of the lake. This trail eventually reaches Chadburn Lake and extra time needs to be budgeted in for this extension.

Hike 4: Chadburn Lake. Medium. Up to 23 km and 1-8 hours return.

NOTE: The Chadburn Lake area has four excellent walking, biking and skiing loops. Maps are found at most major junctions and at the trailhead.

Follow the driving instructions for Hike 1 but stay on the Chadburn Lake Road instead of turning towards the Hidden Lakes/Chadden Lake trailhead. Drive for a further 2 km to a parking area on your right, which is marked by a ski trail sign.

From the map customize a hike or a bike ride into the hills. The red trail is the shortest and easiest, while the blue trail is the longest. They can easily be mixed and matched.

A number of interesting wildflowers can be found in this area. Look for the sweetly-scented pink flowers of wild rose (above) as well as gormans penstemon, a luxurious purple coloured annual. Aromatic sage and juniper also favour the dry south-facing slopes on these hikes.

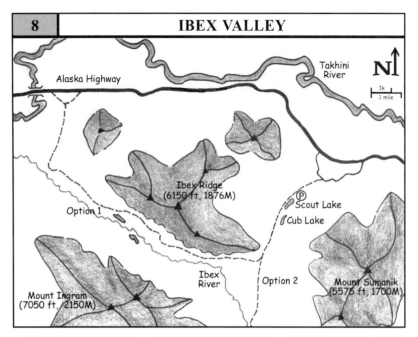

LOGISTICS	MERITS	CONCERNS
Level: Easy **Time:** 1-8 hours **Distance:** Up to 29km **Elev. gain:** 400 feet **Season:** May- Sept. **Maps:** 105 D/11, 12, 13, 14 (Useful for options)	- Gorgeous valley; rock faces, mountains - Lots of potential for a wide variety of activities - Fun for adventurous off-trail hikers	- Some 4x4 traffic - Fairly flat; better to bike than hike this one - Be bear aware - Dog mushers in winter

From Whitehorse follow the Alaska Highway west (towards Haines Junction) for about 19 km. Watch for a sign on your left marking the "Old Alaska Hwy 929-934", about 7 km past the junction with the Klondike Highway. Follow this road for approximately 4 km until a turnoff to Scout Lake Road, marked by a small gravel pit, is reached. Turn left here and follow it for another 4 km. Park at the road junction here. **NOTE:** It is possible to drive further into the valley from here, but a dependable vehicle is required.

Of the two roads in front of you, take the right one that leads uphill. Follow the road for about 5 km until you reach a major junction which was signposted at the time of writing. Take the road on your right to head into the Ibex Valley. Turn back at any point you find convenient or consider the options. Picnicking is excellent on the large granite boulders about 4 km in on the Ibex Valley Road. **NOTE:** Rock climbers are urged to bring rock shoes with them as the 'bouldering' found here can be lots of fun. Remember to always use a spotter.

Option 1: Ibex Valley Loop. Easy. 29 km total and up to 6 hours partial loop. (Biking estimate)

It is possible to make a loop by staying on the Ibex valley road until it reaches the Alaska Highway. This, however, entails some planning such as having a vehicle waiting (Alaska Highway km 1522) or biking the entire circuit, a distance of over 52 km total.

Option 2: Ibex River Road. Easy. Time and distances are variable.

Follow the instructions for the Ibex Valley hike. Turn left instead of right at the junction with the Ibex Valley Road. This old road seems to go on and on and is becoming overgrown and occasionally flooded. Bold explorers may wish to arm themselves with a good map of the area.

More Options: Ibex Ridge/ Mount Ingram. Very Hard. Time and distance variable.

Off-trail hiking enthusiasts will surely enjoy these challenging options which lead to spectacular ridge walks. The Ibex Ridge is best approached from old wood-cutting roads. Try to get high on the ridge as numerous ravines impede efficient progress. It's a little rough at first, but an easy and very scenic ridge walk is the reward . It's best to return by the same general route.

Mount Ingram offers a very challenging ascent, requires some moderate mountaineering skills and is best started from a basecamp. An ice ax is recommended. Cross the Ibex River and then bush-wack to the gently sloping ridge to the south. Follow this ridge up, past dangerously steep ravines and loose talus sections to the summit which is marked by a large rock cairn. Awesome views...

History: Traditionally, this valley had been utilized by First Nations for hunting and traveling purposes. In 1958 a huge fire raged through the area. Myriad access roads found off the main road were used to harvest standing dead wood to keep the Whitehorse homefires burning. Presently, mining activities and the possibility of a pipeline being built through the area have the potential of compromising this northern treasure.

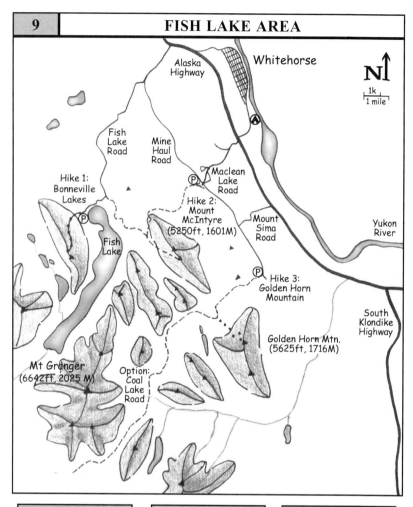

LOGISTICS	MERITS	CONCERNS
Level: Medium-Hard **Time:** 2-10 hours **Distance:** Up to 20 km **Elev. gain:** Up to 2300 feet **Season:** June-Sept. **Maps:** 105 D/11 (Useful)	-Great high country -Lots of options -Fun year-round -Beautiful in fall -Close to town -Biking, skiing in area	-Some motorized activity in area -Horse traffic -Do not remove artifacts -Can be muddy, late snow

Hike 1: Bonneville Lakes. Medium. 7 km and 2-3 hours return.

From downtown Whitehorse drive up 2 Mile Hill (a.k.a. Jack London Boulevard) to the Alaska Highway. Take a right and drive west (towards Haines Junction) for several kilometres. Look for the Kopper King bar and tavern on your left. About 1 km from here turn left onto the Fish Lake Road, which is marked by a sign advertising horse rides.

Follow this increasingly rough road for just over 16 km. At Fish Lake, head right and continue on for about 0.5 km. The unmarked trailhead is on your right and has space for several vehicles.

Follow this dirt trail, which is invariably peppered with hoof prints, up through the forest. The trail is a little eroded at parts with exposed roots. It is a climb of about 1200 feet to a viewpoint overlooking the Bonneville Lakes. From here, numerous options for further exploration exist by heading either right or left from the viewpoint.

Option 1: Fish Lake. Medium. 1-8 km and 1-4 hours return.

From the lake (see above for instructions of how to get there) one can pick up numerous horse trails that follow the lakefront in a clockwise or counterclockwise direction. The trails can get a little vague and/ or muddy at times but in general it's an enjoyable area for strolling and exploring.

NOTE: This whole area has many roads for exploration by foot or, better yet, bike or ski. Consider the Mine Haul Road or the many old roads in the Fish Lake area. Please respect private property and NEVER remove any historical artifacts that may be found.

Hike 2: Mount McIntyre. Medium. 20 km and 6-8 hours return. Elevation gain: 2500ft.

NOTE: Most of this old road can be biked or skied although it has a fairly relentless elevation gain for the first 4 km or so.

From Whitehorse drive up South Access Road (a.k.a. Robert Service Way). Take a left and follow the highway for just under 0.5 km, turning right onto Lobird Road. Take a left, 0.5 km down Lobird, onto Maclean Lake Road. Stay on the main road and park at the T-junction, a little under 3 km up the Maclean Road.

From here take a left and then an immediate right. The road begins to climb steadily and rarely lets up until a wide pass is reached about 5 km later. From here grand views of Fish Lake open up. This is a possible turn-around point.

For those with summit fever continue on the road for another 4 km, staying left at a trail junction about 3 km from the pass.

Follow the road as it gets steeper while looking for a good place to pick a route up to the summit (to your left). Leave the road and pick your way across the subalpine to the summit which is marked by a rock cairn. The road continues to Mount "Mac"s twin summit, which is marked by some communications equipment and presents yet another option. Return by the same route.

Hike 3: Golden Horn Mountain. Hard. 9 km and 5-7 km return.

From Whitehorse drive up South Access Road (a.k.a. Robert Service Way) until you reach the Alaska Highway. Head left and follow it for 6 km until you reach the turnoff for the Mount Sima Ski Hill which is on your right. Follow this road to the ski hill; another 6 km. Continue past the ski hill for just under 1 km. A road on your right leads up towards Golden Horn. You can park at this junction or drive a little ways up if you have a reliable vehicle. The road gets very steep and rough before long.

For the next several km the road gains elevation steeply until the tree-line is reached. The trip to the base of Golden Horn can be quite arduous so prepare yourself mentally. It seems easier to follow the edge of the treeline to the base of the mountain as opposed to slogging through the wet and uneven ground further south. This crossing could take up to two hours. Consider taking a well-deserved break at the base before beginning your ascent to the summit. Picking a route is fairly straight-forward from here. The views are excellent from the top, particularly of Mount Lorne which is found to the south-east. The peak is marked by a cairn and there is ample opportunity for strolling along the wide summit ridge.

Option 2: Coal Lake Road. Medium. Add up to 20 km and 8 hours to Hike 3.

This high ground is very inviting for much of the year. Those looking for an overnight trip in the Whitehorse area may wish to study their maps and customize an adventure. Please practice low impact camping. Instead of heading across the tundra to Golden Horn consider staying on the road. The biking is generally good in this area with a few steep hills to contend with.

The road continues southward toward the Annie Lake area. Numerous other roads split off of the main one and are enticing for further exploration. Also consider bush-wacking across the tundra to numerous local peaks like Mount Granger, the highest in the area.

History: Fish Lake and the surrounding hills has a rich history of human occupation dating at least back to the last glacial retreat in the Southern Yukon some 10 000 years ago. Ancient peoples, travelling from such distant locations as the Pacific coast, the Carcross area, Kusawa Lake and Kluane country, passed through Fish Lake. Evidence of their trading activities remains in the form of native copper heads, Russian iron implements and exotic stone used for tools. Present day outfitter and footpaths pass by prehistoric stone quarries and hunting camps. The caribou herds, dall sheep, bison and moose that sustained these ancient peoples have largely dissapeared from the area following road access in the forties. Traditional fish camps on the lake are still maintained by local natives.

NOTE: Persons finding and considering keeping artifacts should be aware thart this is akin to ripping pages out of a single copy history book of the area. Don't do it! Do, however, keep your eyes open for fossils, ammonites and trilobites from an ancient seabed layer exposed by glaciation.

Skiing near Coal Lake.

Albert Huffenreuter

- 73 -

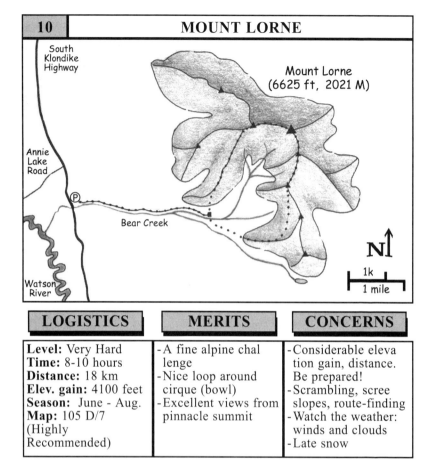

LOGISTICS	MERITS	CONCERNS
Level: Very Hard **Time:** 8-10 hours **Distance:** 18 km **Elev. gain:** 4100 feet **Season:** June - Aug. **Map:** 105 D/7 (Highly Recommended)	- A fine alpine chal lenge - Nice loop around cirque (bowl) - Excellent views from pinnacle summit	- Considerable eleva tion gain, distance. Be prepared! - Scrambling, scree slopes, route-finding - Watch the weather: winds and clouds - Late snow

From downtown Whitehorse drive west on the Alaska Highway to the Carcross cutoff, about 20 km away. Turn right onto the South Klondike Highway and follow it for 18 km. About 2 km past the Annie Lake Road cutoff (which is signposted) on your right, you'll reach a pullover spot on your left. The parking area is on the near side of Bear Creek. Pick up the trail a short way down by the creek.

The trail can be a little confusing at first as it winds its way along the banks of Bear Creek. Try to stay away from the private residences found near here. The trail soon becomes easier to follow and is pleasant to walk on before slowly gaining elevation. Stay right at a trail junction some 4 km in and cross a creek filled with old tin cans. An abandoned cabin found just past here is a possible turn-around point for those desiring a moderate half-day trip, see Option 1.

For those continuing on to the summit pick your way through the bush towards the ridge to the north (left). This section is strenuous and the route a little hard to follow. It becomes more obvious once some elevation is gained. Continue along the ridge as it arcs towards the summit. 'Sidehill' (skirt around lesser peaks) through a challenging section of loose talus before the ridge narrows and some moderate scrambling is required. A number of false peaks will be reached before the true summit. The isolated peak of Mount Lorne provides stunning views and a well-deserved rest area. It is possible to return by this same route, but continuing along the loop is highly recommended.

As you proceed along the mountain spine, more scrambling is required until the route starts to descend through the subalpine. Avoid the temptation to take shortcuts here as they will lead into dense bush with poor visibility. As the main ridge arcs around and down, a braided trail will be encountered. This is a welcome respite from the scree and it will eventually lead you across a creek, back to the cabin and to the trail that follows Bear Creek out to the highway.

Option: Mount Lorne Cabin. Medium. 10 km and 3-4 hours return.

This hike can be customized a number of different ways. Consider travelling up to the cabin for an easy half-day trip. The loop can be done the other way around. Alternatively, some folks may desire to break this loooong day trip up into an overnighter. This will increase comfort as well as safety. Camping is fairly good near the old cabin. Please practise low-impact camping for good karma points.

View Explained: The views from Mount Lorne are some of the finest in the Whitehorse area. Looking to the east lies massive Marsh Lake and south of it Tagish Lake. These 'finger' lakes are leftovers from the massive glaciers that until recently filled this area. These lakes were used by stampeders during the Klondike Goldrush to gain access to the Yukon River, a section of which starts at the end of Marsh Lake.

Looking almost due south one can spy the larger peaks of the Carcross area (see Hikes 11 & 12). The limestone peaks of Gray Ridge lie closer to Mount Lorne to the south-west. Due west lie the sharp summits of the Boundary Range and to the northwest sits the city of Whitehorse. Golden Horn Mountain (Hike # 9:3) is seen almost due north-west and further to the north lies Grey Mountain. From this vantage point Grey Mountain, the closest peak to Whitehorse, looks more like a hill than a mountain.

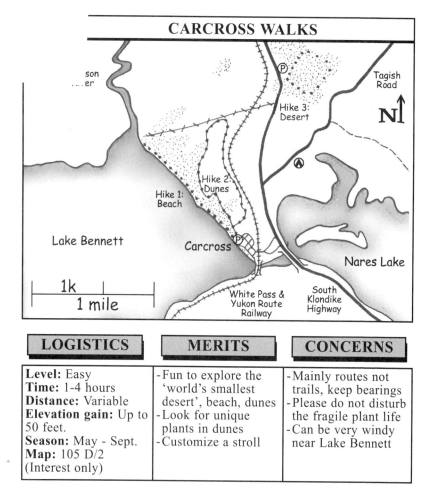

CARCROSS WALKS

son
...er

Tagish
Road

N↑

Hike 3:
Desert

Hike 2:
Dunes

Hike 1:
Beach

Lake Bennett

Carcross

Nares Lake

1k

1 mile

White Pass &
Yukon Route
Railway

South
Klondike
Highway

LOGISTICS	MERITS	CONCERNS
Level: Easy **Time:** 1-4 hours **Distance:** Variable **Elevation gain:** Up to 50 feet. **Season:** May - Sept. **Map:** 105 D/2 (Interest only)	- Fun to explore the 'world's smallest desert', beach, dunes - Look for unique plants in dunes - Customize a stroll	- Mainly routes not trails, keep bearings - Please do not disturb the fragile plant life - Can be very windy near Lake Bennett

Hike 1: Beach. Easy. 4 km and 1 hour return.

Driving south on the South Klondike Highway take a right into Carcross just before the bridge. Follow this road past the Caribou Hotel, across the railroad tracks and towards the waterfront. There is parking and an interpretive sign near the lake and across from the school.

The beach can be followed westward all the way to the mouth of the Watson River some 2 km away. On a nice day it's a treat to remove shoes and socks and wander about. Return by the same route or consider trying to hook onto Hike 2.

Hike 2: Dunes. Easy. 1-10 km and 1-3 hours return.

This area can be accessed near the school, similar to the Hike 1.

There is ample room for exploration as numerous trails (only one is shown) and roads cut through this interesting and beautiful area. Trail descriptions become too complicated so consider making your own route by mixing and matching.

The Watson River, the beach, a power line, the railroad track, local mountains and marked ski trails (three, five and ten km) can all be utilized to find your way. Allow yourself ample time as it is possible to get slightly lost.

Hike 3: Desert. Easy .0.5 km and up to 0.5 hour loop.

The desert can be accessed by walking or driving about 2 km north of Carcross on the South Klondike Highway. The desert is found to the right and is marked by a sign. This general area is fun to explore and it is virtually impossible to get lost.

Options: Those interested in a mountain hike in the Carcross area may wish to check out Mount Montana on the following page. Also consider either Mount Nares or Caribou Mountain. Both peaks are found on the map 105 D/2; a valuable resource if attempting either mountain. The routes up to these summits require route-finding skills and common sense but are relatively easy for those with some experience. In addition the bush-wacking is fairly easy through the sparse forests and the vistas are beautiful and expansive.

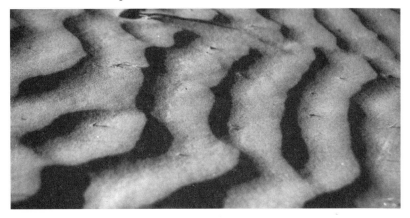

The 'world's smallest desert' is not a real desert at all! The sand and dunes of the area are actually the former shoreline of Bennett Lake.

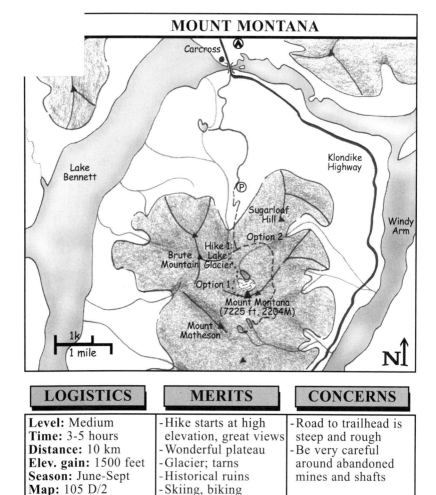

MOUNT MONTANA

Carcross

Lake Bennett

Klondike Highway

Sugarloaf Hill

Option 2

Hike 1:
Brute Lake
Mountain Glacier

Option 1

Mount Montana
(7225 ft, 2204M)

Mount Matheson

Windy Arm

1k
1 mile

N

LOGISTICS	MERITS	CONCERNS

Level: Medium
Time: 3-5 hours
Distance: 10 km
Elev. gain: 1500 feet
Season: June-Sept
Map: 105 D/2
(Recommended)
	-Hike starts at high
	  elevation, great views
	-Wonderful plateau
	-Glacier; tarns
	-Historical ruins
	-Skiing, biking
	  options
		-Road to trailhead is
		  steep and rough
		-Be very careful
		  around abandoned
		  mines and shafts

From the town of Carcross head south, cross the bridge, take the first right and then the next left. Continue up this rough road, if possible, to a pull-over area on the road about 10 km up.

NOTE: A lower portion of the road may be washed out. It may be necessary to add several hours to the hike.

At the ten km point you are right on the edge of the treeline and the views only improve as you follow the road upward. Look into the valley on your right for an old water tower that had once been converted into a Buddhist temple, and, further up, some interesting ruins from a mining operation. About 3 km from the parking spot, the road levels out and splits. The road to the left leads to Option 2; the right leads to Montana's true summit (Option 1).

The peak will be visible from here so head in that direction via the road. After about 2 km of walking on this rough road, the glacier (usually snow-covered) will be visible roughly to the south. A little tarn (alpine lake) nestled below the glacier is a fine destination and turn-around point for a moderate half-day trip, or consider Option 1 which is recommended.

Option 1: Mount Montana Summit. Hard. Add 4 km and 2-3 hours. to Hike 1.

This route leads from the lake (described previously) to the right of the glacier, up to an obvious saddle and then left onto a somewhat steep talus climb up to the summit. The view on a clear day is magnificent.

Option 2: Mount Montana Plateau. Medium. Add up to 22 km and 6 hours to Hike 1.

Turn left at the T-junction at the top of the hill (see first hike) and continue to follow this road as it passes mining bric-a-brac for about 3 km due east, before swinging sharply southward. The road cuts around Mount Montana for several more km. A number of roads spur off the main road. Use your own discretion to find an appropriate one. This old road can be followed an additional 3 or 4 km to some more mining ruins and eventually to a nice little lake. Return by the same route.

More Options! Climb one of the numerous sub-peaks of the Montana massif, follow old mining roads or simply stroll about on the tundra.

Mount Montana in the spring.

13 — FEATHER PEAK

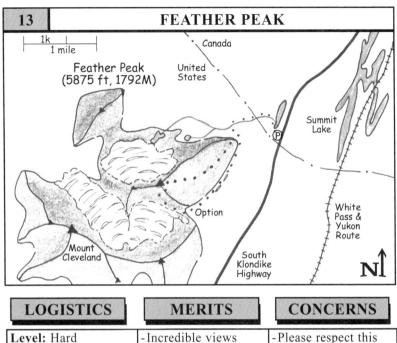

LOGISTICS	MERITS	CONCERNS
Level: Hard **Time:** 5-6 hours return **Distance:** 9 km **Elev. gain:** 2800 feet **Season:** Late June-mid August **Map:** Skagway C/1: US map (Useful)	- Incredible views - Waterfalls and wild flowers - A treat for glacier lovers - Fun area to explore - Bring binoculars	- Please respect this fragile area - Watch the weather; white-outs are common - Some hazards, route-finding, loose rock - Border crossing

From the town of Carcross drive south for 71 km to Canadian Customs. After crossing, drive an additional 12 km to a pull-over on your right, about 1/4 km before the United States-Canada border. "Feather Peak" is the pyramid shaped summit due west.

From the parking area find a steep and rough foot trail that drops down to a creek below. This trail braids; keep left. After crossing the creek by jumping over rocks or wading, follow a trail on the right side of the creek to an attractive little waterfall. Rough trails can be used to gain elevation until another waterfall is reached around 1 km later.

Cross the creek above the second falls. Head in a southerly direction across a splendid alpine meadow; the summit will occasionally come into view. A deep creek bed will be crossed before your route-finding skills will be required. Pick a line towards the peak while being safety conscious around the loose rock and late snow. Some scrambling is unavoidable. **NOTE:** Those wishing a more moderate excursion may wish to stay lower and explore this area.

If you are fortunate to have decent weather, the views upon reaching the top are among the finest featured in this book. Return by the same route or consider Option 1.

Option: Feather Loop. Very Hard. Add 3 km and 2-3 hours.

NOTE: This route passes through some steep and loose scree/ talus slopes and requires a keen route-finding eye. It is recommended for very experienced hikers only.

From the summit pick your way down in an easternly direction before curving southward. The going is slow on the loose rock. Descend gradually in the direction of the glacier and pick your descent line very carefully. Avoid going onto the glacier as crevasses and slick ice pose a serious hazard. Continue downward to the left of the glacier and look for ice caves near the snout.

From here follow the main drainage down while looking for a small pass like area to your left. The walk across some flower-filled meadows beside several small finger-shaped lakes is a particular delight. This route will eventually join the original route you followed up from the highway.

NOTE: Due to the high elevation of the White Pass area and the easy access to the sub-alpine and alpine, much of this area appears to be excellent for off-trail hiking. Unfortunately, the area east of the road is blocked by Summit Lake, and the American side of the Pass drops suddenly and has very little parking. Study the maps to plan a fun adventure.

Quick! Get your camera out before the clouds move in again!

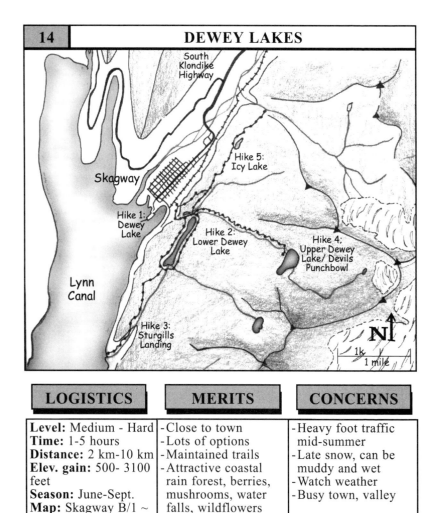

LOGISTICS	MERITS	CONCERNS
Level: Medium - Hard **Time:** 1-5 hours **Distance:** 2 km-10 km **Elev. gain:** 500- 3100 feet **Season:** June-Sept. **Map:** Skagway B/1 ~ US topographical map (Interest only)	-Close to town -Lots of options -Maintained trails -Attractive coastal rain forest, berries, mushrooms, water falls, wildflowers -Some camping by lakes	-Heavy foot traffic mid-summer -Late snow, can be muddy and wet -Watch weather -Busy town, valley

From downtown Skagway walk up Broadway Street to either 3rd or 4th Avenue. Turn right and look for a small footbridge across the railroad tracks that crosses a creek. The trailhead is marked.

Hike 1: Lower Dewey Lake. Medium. 2 km and up to 1 hour return.

Follow this steep trail past several viewing areas. Head right and stay on the main trial, when a junction is encountered. Less than 0.5 km later Lower Dewey Lake is reached. From here many options present themselves.

Hike 2: Lower Dewey Lake Loop. Medium. Add 2 km and 1 hour return to Hike 1.
Simply follow the signs around the lake. A few rough sections.

Hike 3: Upper Dewey Lake/ Devil's Punchbowl. Hard. Add 8 km and 3-4 hours return to Hike 1.
From Lower Dewey Lake follow the signs to Icy Lake/Reid Falls. The trail to Upper Dewey Lake spurs off of the afore-mentioned trail system. The elevation gain is fairly relentless at first as the trail follows switch-backs to the left of Dewey Creek. Eventually the gradient becomes more moderate as a cabin is reached near the lake. This is a possible turn-around point, or consider going on to the Punchbowl.
To complete this extension, plan on adding an hour or two to the total hiking time. This vague trail can be found on the south side of the cabin and is marked by small rock cairns most of the way. Excellent views of Skagway, and the surrounding areas open up as elevation is gained. The trail ends overlooking the tarn (alpine lake) in the Devil's Punchbowl. Return by the same way.

Hike 4: Sturgills Landing. Medium. Add 5 km and 2-3 hours return to Hike 1.
Follow the well-marked trail south towards the Landing. The sometimes muddy trail cuts through what is locally known as the 'Magic Forest' before dropping down to the water via a rocky descent. There is a camping and picnic area at the end of the trail.

Hike 5: Icy Lake. Medium. Add 3 km and 1 hour return to Hike 1.

From Lower Dewey Lake head north (left) along a well-marked but occasionally sketchy trail to the eerie waters of Icy Lake. An impressive stand of massive and fragrant Black Cottonwood trees is found here. It is possible to continue on to Reid Falls from here, but due to all the industrial bric-a-brac found en route, it is not really worth the effort.

History: The name Skagway is of Tlingit origin and means, among other things, "home of the northern wind". Many generations used the nearby Chilkoot Pass as a major trade route into the interior.
William Moore, often credited as the father of Skagway, correctly fore-saw the birth of this coastal town and was promptly marginalised when all hell broke loose during the Klondike Goldrush.
The ragtag town was quickly dominated by a criminal network led by the infamous "Soapy" Smith but has since become a nice little tourist town.

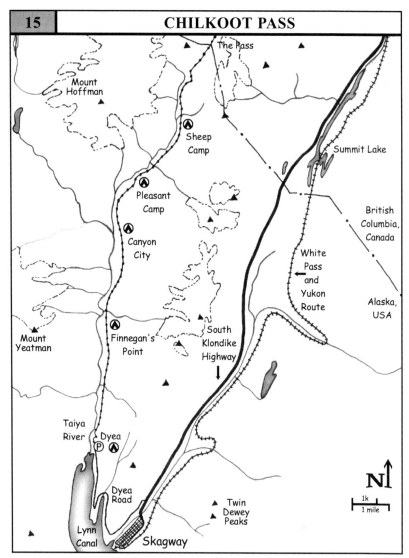

NOTE: This internationally-renowned trail requires solid research and planning. The weather and trail conditions have the potential of being very compromising even to experienced backpackers. Physical conditioning prior to the hike is highly recommended for both comfort and safety.

Be aware that this hike is not a complete loop and hikers should plan their drop-offs and pick-ups well in advance. Consider using shuttle vehicles, bus lines or the train (page174) to get back to Skagway.

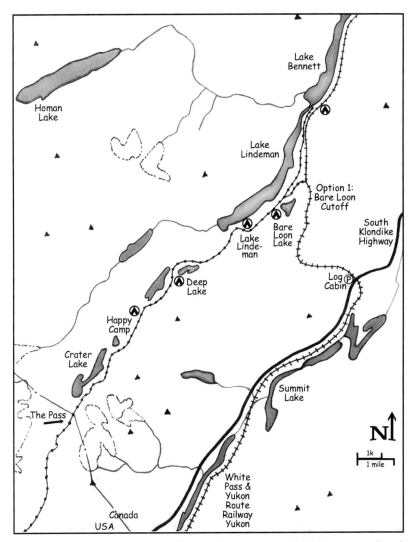

In addition, permits are mandatory; they can be picked up or ordered from Parks Canada or US Parks. See page172. A limited number of hikers are permitted over the pass daily.

It is perfectly possible to do the trail in reverse; in fact there are fewer elevation gains by taking this option. You will, however, be going against the foot traffic instead of with it.

LOGISTICS	MERITS	CONCERNS
Level: Hard **Time:** 3-6 days **Distance:** 53 km + 13 km on railroad tracks back to the highway **Elevation gain:** 3600 feet **Season:** Mid June-late Aug. **Map:** An excellent map can be ordered from Parks Canada, see page 000. Also National Geographic has issued a 1:100,000 trail map (Useful)	- 'Worlds longest museum' - Diverse terrain: coastal rainforest, alpine lakes, boreal forest - Well maintained - Great campsites; a few shelters (day use) - Social; fun; educational - Glaciers; wildflowers; alpine lakes - A fine challenge	- Permits required; book in advance - Can be heavy traffic - Be bear aware - Border crossing - Do not remove artifacts - White-outs and heavy rains - Loose rock, boulders - Late snow and some avalanche danger - Not a complete loop - Campfires prohibited

From Skagway head north on the Southern Klondike Highway for 3.5 km. The well-marked turnoff to Dyea Road is on your left. Follow this somewhat rough road for 13 km to a government-run camping area near the trailhead. A park warden is usually on duty here. The Chilkoot Pass trailhead is found along Dyea Road near the campground.

Section 1) Dyea to Sheep Camp.

The trail begins by following the right side of the Taiya River through lush coastal forest. After some initial elevation gains and losses, the trail becomes more moderate for the next 3 km or so. The often muddy footpath then begins to gain ground slowly, passing a number of campgrounds and historic sites along the way. It can take one or two days to reach Sheep Camp which is 21 km in and is the ideal staging area for the climb over the pass. **NOTE:** Sheep Camp may be full during peak periods.

Section 2) Sheep Camp to Happy Camp (The Pass!).

This is the most challenging section of the trail and requires an early start and reasonable weather. From Sheep Camp the elevation gain is more pronounced until the "Scales" are reached. The "Scales" area, found around the base of the Pass, was once a beehive of activity as many photos from the goldrush era illustrate.

Low clouds, large boulders, late snow, avalanches and an elevation grade of almost forty five degrees are a few of the concerns facing the modern adventurer. The trail becomes more of a route and is marked by wands and cairns. Be prepared to stop or be stopped at Canada Customs upon reaching the top of the pass; permits and I.D. will likely be checked here.

Once through the narrow notch that is the "summit", the bulk of the elevation has been gained. Congratulations, it's almost all downhill from here. The trail follows to the right of a number of gorgeous alpine lakes before Happy Camp is reached 7 km from the pass.

The Scales were located at the base of the steepest part of the pass.

It was here that goods were weighed on scales and packed for the demanding hike up the notch to the US/ Canada border. In winter 1897 the North-West Mounted Police posted on top of the col watched an unending line of people, cloaked in swirling snow, assault this deadly pass time and time again. Many stampeders made over 50 trips up and back down to the Scales to relay their required 1000 pounds of supplies.

Section 3) Happy Camp to Lake Bennett.

From here the trail continues to cut through the subalpine environment slowly losing elevation. Those with lots of time, energy and supplies may consider exploring this incredible area. In addition, budget in some time looking over the interpretive material at the Lake Lindeman Campsite and warden station.

The trail passes some waterfalls before reaching Bare Loon Lake campground, and just past it the shortcut to the northern trailhead (see Option 1). It is, however, much more interesting to continue on to Lake Bennett and finish the entire length of this historic route. The final section of the trail passes through some rolling sand dunes before majestic Lake Bennett is reached. A visit to the oft photographed wooden church nearby is very worthwhile.

From here one can hop on the train back to Skagway (book ahead, page 174) or hike out to the Klondike Highway (Log Cabin) via a 13 km and 3-4 hour stretch along the railway. This last choice is the most popular and the most tedious option.

Option: Bare Loon Cutoff. Easy. 9 km and 2-3 hours.

This spur trail shaves over 5 km off of the total trail length and an another 4 km from the walk out along the railroad that leads back to the highway.

The Tlingit were the original developers and travelers of the famous Chilkoot Pass. They jealously guarded their trade route, used for mil-

E.A. Hegg Collection

lennia, to trade dried fish, fish oils, shells and other commodities to the inland native people, primarily the Tutchone and Tagish.

During the goldrush it was impossible to stop the flood of newcomers to their lands, and many Tlingit went to work as packers. Before long they had earned a reputation of being able to carry immense loads. However, this valuable service was soon rendered virtually obsolete when a tramway was built in 1899 near the Chilkoot summit.

The Tlingit today are found around Skagway, Haines and Juneau, Alaska as well as Atlin, BC and parts of the Southern Yukon.

CHAPTER 4

KLUANE REGION

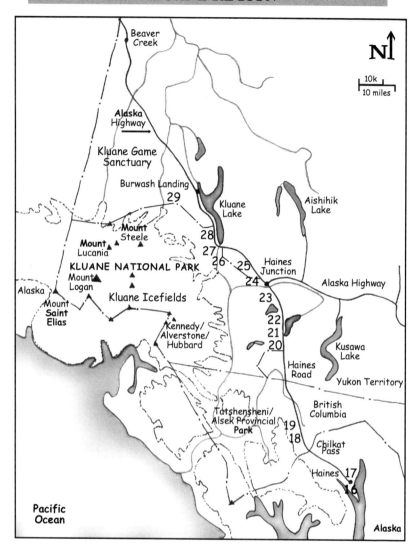

16. Mount Ripley	21. Cottonwood Trails	26. Slims River Valley
17. Mount Ripinski	22. Kathleen Lake	27. Sheep Mountain
18. Chilkat Pass Area	23. Auriol Trail	28. Kluane Lake
19. Samuel Glacier	24. Haines Junction	29. Burwash Loop
20. South Kluane Park	25. Mount Decoeli	

The Land: Kluane National Park, a Unesco World Heritage site, contains all of Canada's loftiest summits. The immense glaciation in the interior of the park is part of the largest non-polar icefield in the world and home to Mount Logan, the elusive giant that is Canada's highest peak. Amazingly, on the edge of the ice age live a variety of Canada's largest mammals like the dall sheep, mountain goats, moose and the awesome grizzly bear.

To the south lies the new Tatshenshini/Alsek Provincial Park and the Chilkat Pass region. Wildflowers, glaciers, and wildlife are all common in this dramatic area. This region is the traditional and present home of the Tlingit, Tutchone and Upper Tanana people.

Finally, at the end of the road lies beautiful Haines, Alaska. High in the sky enormous peaks and glaciers show their presence. In the valleys, lush coastal rainforests are filled with berries and mushrooms. This place really engages the senses.

Walking and Hiking: Kluane National Park is truly a wilderness park. Trails are barely developed and many places are rarely visited. The challenges of hiking in the region can be amply rewarded by views of the "Monsters", Canada's highest peaks, huge valley glaciers and the massive Kluane icefields. Short interpreted walks in the park are also available. Wildlife abounds and one needs to be very bear aware. Registration is mandatory for overnight trips. See page 172 for more information on Kluane National Park.

Chilkat Pass has exceptional hiking on clear days, which, unfortunately, can be fairly rare. Glaciers are close to the road and wildflowers can erupt into bloom around the middle of summer.

Haines, Alaska, has a lot to offer to outdoor enthusiasts, such as easy beach strolls, several challenging alpine hikes, superb scenery, sea-kayaking and more.

Concretions aka "Nature's bowling balls" are occaisonally spotted in Kluane National Park and other areas of the Yukon.

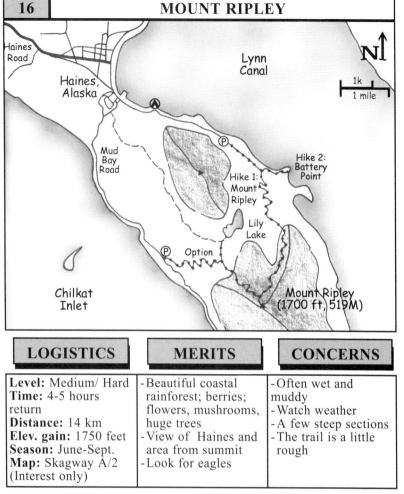

LOGISTICS	MERITS	CONCERNS
Level: Medium/ Hard **Time:** 4-5 hours return **Distance:** 14 km **Elev. gain:** 1750 feet **Season:** June-Sept. **Map:** Skagway A/2 (Interest only)	-Beautiful coastal rainforest; berries; flowers, mushrooms, huge trees -View of Haines and area from summit -Look for eagles	-Often wet and muddy -Watch weather -A few steep sections -The trail is a little rough

From the town of Haines get onto (or stay on) the Haines Road. Follow it to the waterfront where it turns into the Beach Road. This road passes a campground (specifically for non-motorized travelers) and a subdivision. Park where the road ends, about 4 km from the centre of town. The trailhead is marked.

This footpath leads through a lush forest until, about 2 km in, a signposted trail junction is encountered. Turning left leads to the beach (Hike 2). Turn right here for Mount Riley. The trail, which at the time of writing was a little rough in sections, begins a fairly steady gain as it meanders upwards. The summit and the viewing station are reached approximately 5 km from the beach junction. Return by the same route or consider the option below.

Option: Mud Bay Loop. Medium/ Hard. About the same time and distance as the first half of Hike 1.

NOTE: Mount Ripley's summit may be reached this way, or else consider making a loop by dropping down to Mud Bay Road and then back to town via this spur trail. You may wish to have a vehicle waiting at this trailhead.

From the summit of Mount Ripley return on the trail on which you came up. Turn left at the first trail junction (signposted at time of writing) less than ½ km from the summit. A steep and somewhat gnarly series of switchbacks await the intrepid hiker. Turn right at the Mud Bay Road and follow it until it ends about 4 km later. Turn left to go back to Haines, or turn right to the Beach Road and the previous hike's trailhead.

Hike 2: Battery Point Beach. Medium. 6 km and 2-3 hours return.

From the first trail junction (Hike 1) pick up this spur trail that leads to the beach. Walk along a rocky stretch of beach before reaching a nice viewing area. It is possible to continue and explore the waterfront from this point. This area is very attractive and well worth a visit.

The bald eagle is a common sight in the Haines area. This magnificent raptor likes to live by water and is highly skilled at fishing. It is a social creature, and sometimes shares a roost with up to several dozen individuals.

A very vocal bird, the bald eagle is usually spotted high up in trees keeping a stern eye on the general area.

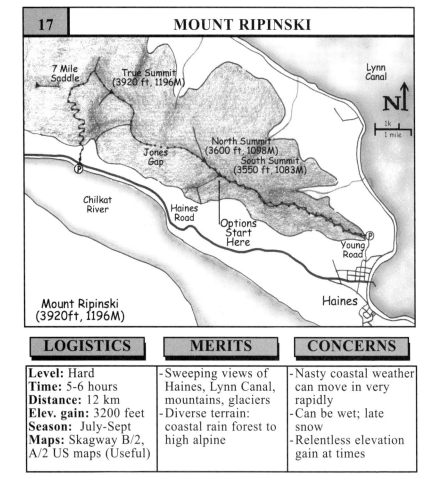

17	MOUNT RIPINSKI

Mount Ripinski
(3920ft, 1196M)

LOGISTICS	MERITS	CONCERNS
Level: Hard **Time:** 5-6 hours **Distance:** 12 km **Elev. gain:** 3200 feet **Season:** July-Sept **Maps:** Skagway B/2, A/2 US maps (Useful)	- Sweeping views of Haines, Lynn Canal, mountains, glaciers - Diverse terrain: coastal rain forest to high alpine	- Nasty coastal weather can move in very rapidly - Can be wet; late snow - Relentless elevation gain at times

Drive, walk or bike along Second Avenue (a.k.a. Young Street) for over 2 km from downtown Haines. Ignore two turnoffs to your right. The road begins to pass a new subdivision before becoming a little rough. The marked trail head, found on your left, is just past a construction area and can be a little tricky to spot. This trail, which begins as an old road, starts flat but soon begins to climb quite steadily through the lush forest. A number of viewing areas and possible turn-around points are reached on the way up to the treeline. Eventually you will pop into the subalpine and marvellous views will be the reward for your toils. The South Summit of Ripinski (3550 feet) is the first major viewpoint to be reached. Return by the same route or consider the options.

Option 1: North Summit. Hard. Add 1 km and up to 1 hour return to previous hike.

From the South Summit consider hiking over to the next summit (3600 feet) which allows for slightly improved views of the area.

Option 2: Jones Gap. Very Hard. Add 10 km and 4 hours return.

It is possible to reach the true summit of Ripinski (3920 feet) via this route and then backtracking. Other possibilities include looping back to the highway via 7 mile saddle (Option 3) or starting the entire hike at the north trailhead also mentioned in Option 3.

From the north summit pick your way down to the large saddle to the north-west which then leads steeply up to the true summit. NOTE: There are steep, wet sections, numerous switchbacks and vague trail sections on this option.

Option 3: Seven Mile Saddle. Very Hard. 5 km and 3 hours to highway.

From the true summit pick your way down a very steep section to a small saddle to the west. A number of springs with cool refreshing water can be found around here. Next, follow another steep switchback trail section which will eventually drop down to the Haines Road.

It is recommended that if you choose this option that you have a vehicle waiting as your capacity for walking at this point will likely be seriously reduced. To get to the north trailhead drive just before Milepost 7, north on the Haines Road. Look for the rifle range, a trail signpost and a boardwalk on your right. There is limited parking opposite the trailhead.

View Explained: From any one of the summits of Mount Ripinski amazing vistas open up. The Chilkat and Chilkoot Inlets are visible to the west and east of Ripinski respectively. They empty into the Lynn Canal and eventually into the Pacific Ocean. Look for 'floating hotels' (ferries) which look like children's toys from this vantage point.

Numerous glaciers can be seen grinding their way down to the water from the Takhinsha and Chilkat Ranges to the south and east. Haines is clearly seen from here, as well as the Taiya Inlet, the canal to the northeast, which leads to Skagway. Also look for the green rounded summit of Mount Riley (Hike # 16), seen to the south-east just behind the town of Haines.

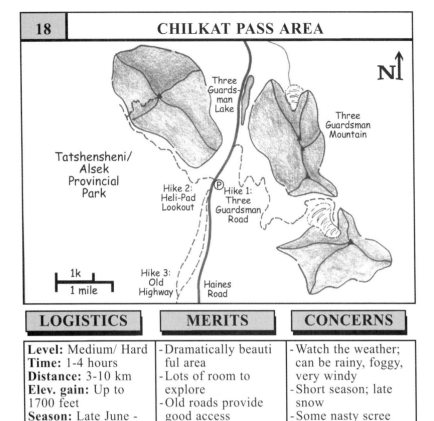

Three
Guards-
man
Lake

N↑

Three
Guardsman
Mountain

Tatshensheni/
Alsek
Provincial
Park

Hike 2:
Heli-Pad
Lookout

Ⓟ Hike 1:
Three
Guardsman
Road

1k
1 mile

Hike 3:
Old
Highway

Haines
Road

LOGISTICS	MERITS	CONCERNS
Level: Medium/ Hard **Time:** 1-4 hours **Distance:** 3-10 km **Elev. gain:** Up to 1700 feet **Season:** Late June - mid Aug. **Map:** 114 P/9 (Useful)	- Dramatically beautiful area - Lots of room to explore - Old roads provide good access - Great views	- Watch the weather; can be rainy, foggy, very windy - Short season; late snow - Some nasty scree and glaciers; be cautious if exploring - Unmaintained roads

Drive south from Haines Junction for 159 km, or north from Haines, Alaska, for 90 km on the Haines Road. If coming from Canada look for Three Guardsman Lake, which is signposted and found on the left side of the road. There is a large pull-over area about 1 km past the far end of the lake, and highway marker # 90 is nearby. Park here, or consider parking near km 92 (the lake) if doing Hike 1.

Hike 1: Three Guardsman Mountain Satellite. Medium/ Hard. 10 km, 3-4 hours return and 1700 feet elevation gain.
The first section of this hike requires some route-finding skills. From the parking area at km 90, follow the highway north on foot for about 1 km. Pick your way down to a creek (to your right) that parallels the highway. Cross it and work your way towards the old road which should be visible cutting up along the side of the mountain. The first section is badly overgrown, but soon opens up and walking becomes very enjoy-

able for the next number of km. As elevation is gained, the road leads through a series of switchbacks to some nice subalpine meadows. Turn around at any point along this road, or consider the following option.

Option: Guardsman Summit. Very Hard. Add 4 km, 3 hours and 1500 feet elevation gain.

As the road circles around towards the south, a nasty, steep ridge with rust-coloured rocks comes into view. This ridge requires extreme care to ascend; be aware of loose rock and avoid the steep snow-covered glacier to your left as the runout is particularly dangerous. The summit views are sublime and it is possible to make a loop by descending down to the access road via the wide ridge to the west.

Hike 2: "Heli-Pad Viewpoint". Medium/ Hard. 9 km, 3-4 hours return and 1800 feet elevation gain.

An old road leads to a spectacular 360 degree view of the Coastal Mountains, marred only by a heli-pad found on the summit.

From the parking area (Hike 1) cross the road and walk northward. The rough road, on your right, is a little tricky to spot and begins very steeply. (How vehicles ever got up it is beyond me!)

After several km of heading up, the road evens a bit and crosses through a boggy meadow; stay to the right here. After the meadow, the road splits; stay right again. As you begin to climb up the side of the mountain and past some lovely alpine flowers, a number of orange wands and rock cairns are encountered. Follow these to the summit. NOTE: Please do not tamper with the equipment found here.

Return by the same route or, if your route-finding skills are sharp, try to pick your way down the east side of the mountain.

Hike 3: Old Highway. Medium/ Hard. 4 km and 1-2 hours loop.

Two sections of the old highway can be connected to make a loop with little elevation gain and loss. From the parking area (see Hike 1) cross the road, walk south and look for two old roads that parallel the highway. At the time of writing they were marked by a brown BC Parks sign prohibiting motorized vehicles. Take the top road and follow it southward.

The road becomes increasingly vague and overgrown, but is still discernable until it hits a creek . Cross this creek and pick up the other section of the old road. Turn left and simply head back to the trailhead.

It is possible to follow the old highway down for a total of 14 km where it rejoins the Haines Road but this is heavy bear and moose habitat.

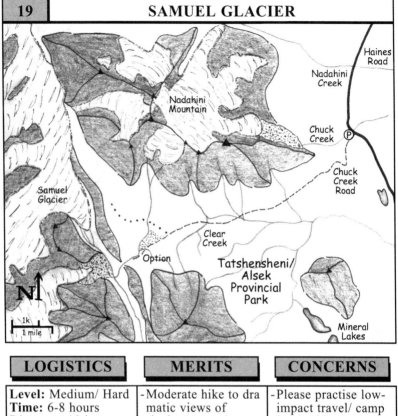

LOGISTICS	MERITS	CONCERNS
Level: Medium/ Hard **Time:** 6-8 hours **Distance:** 19 km **Elev. gain:** 700 feet **Season:** Late June-mid Aug **Map:**114 P/10 (May be useful)	-Moderate hike to dramatic views of glacier 'snouts' -Wildflowers, open views -In a word: Spectacular!	-Please practise low-impact travel/ camping in this area -Can be very muddy -1 major creek crossing; many smaller creeks -Watch the weather

Drive 142 km south on the Haines Road from the town of Haines Junction, (38 km south of the BC/ Yukon border). The trail can also be reached by driving 107 km north from Haines, Alaska.

Look for a sign marking Chuck Creek on your right (if driving south). There is also a big, brown BC Parks sign near here. Park on the far (south) side of the creek. The old road can be seen to your left by following the creek up for a short distance.

This old road, which is steep and often quite wet near the beginning, begins to ascend for the first km or so. A moderate gradient is encountered for the remainder of the way. Numerous small creeks will be crossed en route. About 6 km in, the only major hazard, Clear Creek, will have to be forded. See page 42 for creek crossing tips. Less than a km from here the creek will be crossed again before passing through a soggy subalpine area. It is possible to bypass the creek via a nasty bushwack.

The road gets increasingly vague. Leave it at this point and head towards the mountain directly ahead of you. A large washout should be on your left as you approach a nice viewing area to the west. By heading up slightly and veering north, amazing views of several glacier snouts come into view. If time and energy permits, it is possible to continue exploring in this general direction.

Option: Chuck Creek Road. Medium. Time and distance variable.

Although I've only hiked a portion of it, it is possible to continue on the old road by keeping to the left (south) of the washout. It is rumoured that the remains of an abandoned gypsum mine can be found further along the road.

NOTE: This area has lots of room to explore, but do be aware of several limiting factors such as an impassable creek and canyon near the lowest glacier snout. Also try to avoid bushwacking through the backbrush around here as it can be positively evil. Have fun!

Hiker near the snout of the awesome Samuel Glacier.

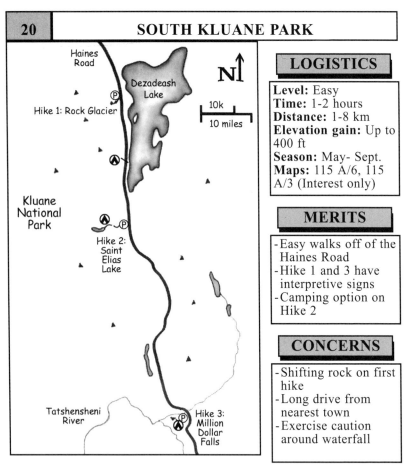

LOGISTICS

Level: Easy
Time: 1-2 hours
Distance: 1-8 km
Elevation gain: Up to 400 ft
Season: May- Sept.
Maps: 115 A/6, 115 A/3 (Interest only)

MERITS

- Easy walks off of the Haines Road
- Hike 1 and 3 have interpretive signs
- Camping option on Hike 2

CONCERNS

- Shifting rock on first hike
- Long drive from nearest town
- Exercise caution around waterfall

Hike 1: Rock Glacier.   Easy. 1 km and ½ hour return.

The marked trailhead is found on the right side of the Haines Road, 44 km south of Haines Junction.

Follow the trail across a foot bridge, past some interpretive panels and up a rocky trail to a viewing area of the massive Dezedeash Lake. Return by the same route or, if feeling adventurous, venture out further onto the Rock Glacier. Several routes can be found from here. Please be aware of loose rock. Bring some binoculars to try and spy the mountain goats which like this area. Mountain scramblers may wish to ascend nearby ridge systems.

Hike 2: St. Elias Lake.   Easy. 8 km and 2-3 hours return.

This hike can be found 60 km south of Haines Junction on the Haines

Road. Look for the marked trailhead which is found on your right.

This old road, which has signs posted part-way, follows up and down a few small hills to the banks of Saint Elias Lake. A trail junction is found just over 1 km in; keep to the right here.

A primitive camp is found at the lake which includes a fire/cooking area, a bear cache and a few flat spots to set up the tent. Please register with Parks Canada in Haines Junction if staying a night or two. Nearby peaks invite the well-prepared, off-trail hiker. Look for vague game trails around the lake.

Hike 3: Million Dollar Falls.   Easy. ½ km and ½ hour loop.

This campground trail is found 89 km down the Haines Road from Haines Junction, 14 km before the BC/ Yukon border.

The trailhead can be found near the picnic area and camp shelter. Several interpretive signs explain the history of the area and the origin of the falls' peculiar name. It's best to stay on the official trails as the unofficial trails look loose and eroded. It is a very short trail, but the river, falls and general area are nice places to relax after logging some hours on the Haines Road.

The mighty moose is occasionally seen in this general region.

- The moose is the largest member of the deer family.
  - The moose provides an important food source for many of the areas carnivores and omnivores.
    - Moose defend themselves from predators with their antlers and hooves.
    - Adult males (bulls) can weigh up to 1700 pounds!
    - Moose found in the Territory are often a mix of two sub-species, the Alaskan moose and the woodland moose.

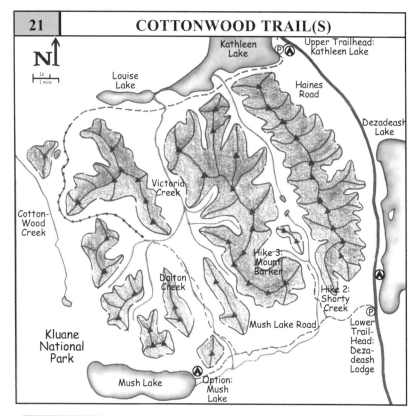

LOGISTICS	MERITS	CONCERNS

Level: Medium/ Hard
Time: 4-6 days
Distance: 78 km
Elev. gain: 1700 feet
Season: June-August
Maps: 115/ A/11, 12,
115 A/5, A/6
(May be useful)
	- Well marked and
	  maintained; popular
	- Nice, primitive
	  camping areas
	- Good views of
	  frontal range
	- No big elevation
	  gains
		- Be VERY bear aware
		- Some creek cross
		  ings; one fairly
		  major one (Victoria)
		- Not a full loop
		- Registration
		  mandatory

NOTE: This semi-loop can be started at either end. Registration and the use of bear canisters is mandatory for overnight trips. Some camping sites may be closed due to bear activity and high creek levels may pose a considerable hazard.

I have only hiked and skied portions of this trail; the following information is supplemented with written and first-hand accounts. Although the hike is marked by signs and markers the whole way you may want to ask Parks Canada about current trail conditions.

From Haines Junction drive south on the Haines Road to either one of the two trailheads.

Upper Trailhead (Kathleen Lake): Located 32 km south of Haines Junction. Turn right and drive past the campground and down to the lake front.

Lower Trailhead (Dezedeash Lodge): Located 55 km south of Haines Junction. Turn right here and park at the abandoned lodge or consider driving up this rough road a short distance. If the gate is open, it is possible to drive a number of kilometres up the Mush Lake Road. This hike described below starts from here.

Section 1) Lower Trailhead to Dalton Pass.

From the lower trailhead, follow the Mush Lake Road for a total of 16 km. The trail splits several km in; take either option. Keep left at the marked junction at km 5.5 and be prepared to cross Alder Creek just past here; follow markers downstream.

Several more creeks must be crossed; look for obscured bridges to your right. Another trail junction is encountered at km 16. Take a right here.

NOTE: Due to bear activity in this area it seems best to avoid camping around here.

The trail steeply follows Dalton Creek until Dalton Pass is reached about 5 km up. Peaks in the area provide good views and are generally quite easy to climb. Consider climbing the mountain due west from here.

Section 2) Dalton Pass to Victoria Pass.

Follow the creek that flows down from Dalton Pass until it joins Victoria Creek some 5 km from Dalton Pass. This last section follows some steep switchbacks and numerous small creek crossings. Take out the binoculars and look around; a variety of wildlife sightings are a common occurrence here.

Look for markers in this area to cross Victoria Creek. Continue west and follow the creek upstream for 4 km until you reach Victoria Pass. Avoid going up the two creeks that flow into Victoria Creek. Numerous footpaths and hard-to-spot wooden markers make this area a little tricky to get through. The most important junction is about 3 km from the first crossing of Victoria Creek. Stay on the footpath, to your right (northwest), and avoid following the road any further. A steep elevation gain of about 500 feet takes you to the top of Victoria Pass, the second and final pass of this hike. Look for markers and rock cairns and consider exploring this area before elevation is lost as you descend into the Cottonwood Valley.

Section 3) Cottonwood Valley to Lake Louise.

The trail drops down to the wide valley from Victoria Pass, circles west around a peak and then heads due north. Stay on the near side of Cottonwood Creek and look for markers downstream that guide you along the creek and occasionally into some thickets nearby.

From this point the trail starts to head north and enters a wide meadow. An easily spotted marker at km 49 is a good place to camp, the best for the next five km.

The meadow can be wet and boggy, but fear not, the old road is soon regained. The road leads past the old "Johobo" minesite which is found on your left. The camping is fairly good in this area. Camp here or walk an additional 7 km to Lake Louise.

Section 4) Louise and Kathleen Lakes to Upper Trailhead.

Continue to follow the road/ footpath eastward passing above Louise Lake and past a number of steep slopes and small creeks. Once at the far end of Louise Lake you will encounter the cold and swift water of Victoria Creek. This creek is best crossed in the morning, near the lake, and is often the most challenging part of this hike. See page 42 for creek crossing tips.

After about 3 km the trail returns to thick forest before reaching the shores of majestic Kathleen Lake. Goat Creek, which offers a nice primitive campsite, will have to be crossed and can be tricky. Look for the high trail that starts to cut along the mountain that lines Kathleen Lake; avoid the older, lower trail that follows closer to the lake. Soon a junction with the King's Throne hike will be encountered. It is now a short walk of 2 km to the campground at Kathleen Lake and the end of the hike. Congratulations!

Option: Mush Lake Road. Easy. 22 km to lake (44 km return) and 1-3 days return.

NOTE: This makes for a better biking than hiking trip.

Instead of following the Cottonwood trail, consider a trip to Mush Lake and the rustic campground situated there. Follow the instructions for the Cottonwood trail; simply stay left at every marked trail junction until you reach the lake and a nice simple campground. There are some steep hills in the last third of the trip.

Hike 2: Shorty Creek. Medium. Up to 21 km and 5-6 hours return from Cottonwood lower trailhead.

This a nice, moderate day hike in the Cottonwood area. Hike, bike, or possibly drive to the marked trail junction 5.5 km down Mush Lake Road (driving will knock off a total of 11 km and 2-3 hours from the total distance and time). Turn right here and follow the road for an additional 1 km, keeping left where the road splits. Park here, or continue on foot or bike across the suspension bridge that spans Alder Creek.

Within 1 km the road begins to rise sharply for several km before dropping down to another creek, see Hike 3 (below). Continue on the road until it ends at Shorty Creek about 5 km from the suspension bridge. Turn around here or follow a rough route upstream along the left side of Shorty Creek to the ruins of an old mining camp about 1 km up.

Springtime near Shorty Creek.

Hike 3: Mount Barker. Very Hard. 16 km and 8-10 hours return from suspension bridge. Elevation gain: 4000 feet.

Follow the Shorty Creek Road for 3.5 km from the bridge. After the road begins to descend follow an unnamed creek that climbs steadily up for 3 km to a plateau area with several small picturesque lakes.

Mount Barker is the summit to the north of the lakes. It is a steep talus scramble, an elevation gain of 1000 feet; to stunning views of the icefields. **NOTE:** This is a rarely visited area and has considerable bear activity; make lots of noise while following the creek.

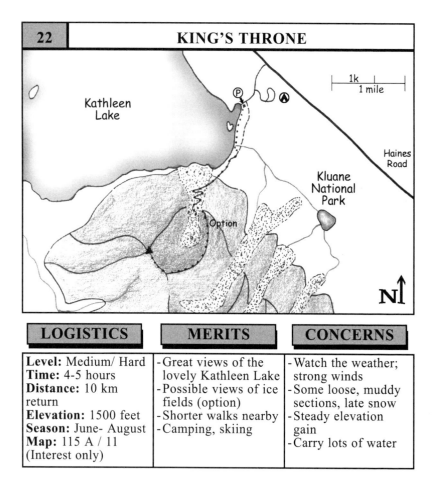

LOGISTICS	MERITS	CONCERNS
Level: Medium/ Hard **Time:** 4-5 hours **Distance:** 10 km return **Elevation:** 1500 feet **Season:** June- August **Map:** 115 A / 11 (Interest only)	- Great views of the lovely Kathleen Lake - Possible views of ice fields (option) - Shorter walks nearby - Camping, skiing	- Watch the weather; strong winds - Some loose, muddy sections, late snow - Steady elevation gain - Carry lots of water

From Haines Junction drive south on the Haines Road for 32 km. Turn right at the Kathleen Lake Campground and drive down to the waterfront.

From near the camp shelter, look for the start of the trail/road which is marked by a few Parks signs and a gate. Follow this rough road for 1 km to a trail junction. (**NOTE:** Alternatively, the beach, which roughly parallels the old road, can be followed, although getting onto the King's Throne trail from here may take a little trial-and-error.) Take a left at the Cottonwood/ King's Throne junction. The footpath begins to gain in elevation as a number of switchbacks are reached. Look for rock cairns and please stay on the main trail to avoid erosion. Views improve as the treeline is passed. The rock glacier, which resembles a mighty monarch's royal throne, is arrived at after an elevation gain of 1500 feet. Turn around here, explore the giant cirque or consider the Option.

Option: King's Throne Summit. Very Hard. Add 5 km, 3 hours and up to 2000 feet elevation gain to Hike 1.

NOTE: This can be a grueling hike and is not recommended if the slope is slick and icy or the weather unstable.

Looking at the mountain (away from the lake), take the steep ridge to your left (south). After throwing your cardio-vascular system into over-drive for about 1 hour the summit ridge is reached. Views into the ice-fields are possible on a clear day. Return along the same route or "bag" the peak, almost 1 km to the northwest.

NOTE: Those with strong scrambling skills may wish to follow the cirque ridge down from the summit, but this is generally not recommended as it is very steep and often icy.

Hike 2: Kathleen Lake Waterfront.   Easy. Up to 2 km, and up to 1 hour return.

A number of easy walks can be found in the Kathleen Lake area. Consider walking the Kokanee Trail which starts at the waterfront/camp shelter and follows the lake past numerous interpreted signs. The section of beach that leads to the King's Throne can also be followed for an hour's easy stroll.

NOTE: For those desiring a longer trip in the area with little elevation gain consider walking a stretch of the Cottonwood Trail (pages 102-105) that parallels Kathleen Lake. A rustic campground is found at km 8; registration is mandatory for overnight trips.

'Klondike Nudist Club' on a winter outing on Kathleen Lake.

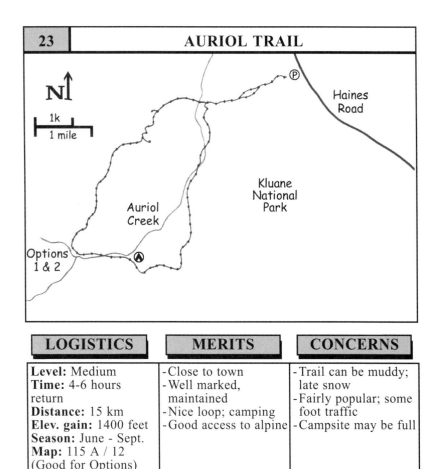

LOGISTICS | MERITS | CONCERNS

LOGISTICS	MERITS	CONCERNS
Level: Medium **Time:** 4-6 hours return **Distance:** 15 km **Elev. gain:** 1400 feet **Season:** June - Sept. **Map:** 115 A / 12 (Good for Options)	- Close to town - Well marked, maintained - Nice loop; camping - Good access to alpine	- Trail can be muddy; late snow - Fairly popular; some foot traffic - Campsite may be full

NOTE: The trailhead and some guidebooks claim this is a 19 km hike; in reality it is much closer to 15 km.

From Haines Junction head south on the Haines Road for just over 7 km. The trailhead on your right is clearly marked. Park here.

Follow the trail to a 1 km marker where the path splits and then connects again shortly. At the 2.8 km marker the loop begins. The right side is steeper and leads past several viewing stations; the left is more moderate. A nice, basic campground (3 tent sites, outhouse and bear cache) is located at the halfway point of the loop and is great for a lunch break or overnight camping. The brush at the top section of the loop thins out considerably, allowing for good views and access to the alpine.

Option 1: Auriol Bowl. Hard. Add 3-4 km and 2-3 hours return.

Those with some route-finding skills may enjoy exploring this fascinating area. About 1 km past the campground, if you took the left side of the loop, the trail crosses over a small wooden bridge. This creek is marked by a wooden marker at km 8.2; the creek leads towards a large glacier-carved bowl to the west. (NOTE: Use this marker to reconnect to the Auriol trail on your return.)

Follow the creek, game trails and/or bushwack to reach the interior of the bowl which is filled with moraine deposits. A number of colourful glacier lakes can be found here. The whole bowl is open for exploration as well as the surrounding peaks. See Option 2.

Option 2: Quill Peak/ Unnamed Peak. Very Hard. Add 4-6 km and 6-8 hours to the first hike and Option 1.

Summits to the south and north of Auriol Bowl can be accessed from Option 1. The unnamed peak to the north is for scree lovers only and includes one very steep section.

Obvious routes to the south lead to what is locally known as Quill Peak, an ice-capped summit with outstanding views. Once again, this involves a long, rocky ascent and a steep, icy section that leads to the summit. A long ice axe is recommended on both routes as well as a good dose of common sense.

View Explained: The two viewing stations found on the north (right at the junction) section of the Auriol loop are great places to view the Shakwak Trench and area. Observe the dramatic differences between the jagged peaks of the Frontal Range and the softer, rounded mountains across the valley, the Ruby Range. The Shakwak Trench, that seperates ther ranges, represents a major fault line and contains many lakes.

Look due north to see Haines Junction and behind it the rocky bluffs of Paint Mountain. Pine Lake is nestled to the southeast of Paint Mountain. Looking further to the east look for examples of hanging and U-shaped valleys.

Other Options: Those desiring a multi-day trip into the Auriol Range may wish to consider the Quill Creek hike that starts at km 17 of the Haines Road. This 2-3 day route leads up the creek, through a canyon and eventually up to a high plateau with great views into the park. Contact Parks Canada in Haines Junction for more information.

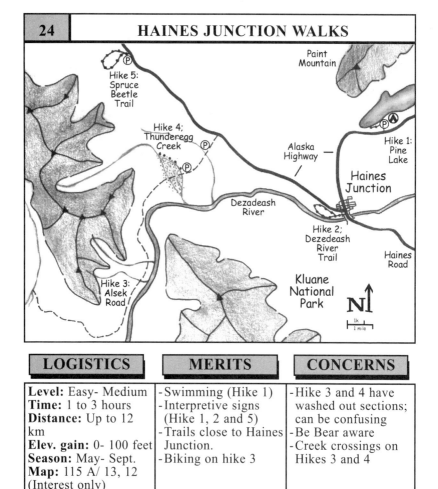

LOGISTICS	MERITS	CONCERNS
Level: Easy- Medium **Time:** 1 to 3 hours **Distance:** Up to 12 km **Elev. gain:** 0- 100 feet **Season:** May- Sept. **Map:** 115 A/ 13, 12 (Interest only)	-Swimming (Hike 1) -Interpretive signs (Hike 1, 2 and 5) -Trails close to Haines Junction. -Biking on hike 3	-Hike 3 and 4 have washed out sections; can be confusing -Be Bear aware -Creek crossings on Hikes 3 and 4

Hike 1: Pine Lake. Easy. 1 km and up to ½ hour return.

The Pine Lake Campground is found 7 km out of Haines Junction on the Alaska Highway and is marked by a sign.

Follow the campground road down to the beach. The swimming and dipping can be, shall we say, refreshing... on hot summer days. This short trail begins to the left of the beach. Follow it past numerous interpretive panels to a lookout of the lake and Paint Mountain.

Hike 2: Dezadeash River Loop. Easy. 4 km and 1-2 hours loop.

From the centre of Haines Junction walk or drive south towards the bridge on the Haines Road. The marked trailhead is on the right just before the bridge. This trail can also be started across the road from the

Park Centre behind the RV campground gas station.

This well maintained trail leads past a number of interpretive signs before reaching a junction. Stay on the main trail (left and away from the RV campground) and follow it to a wooden viewing station overlooking the Dezadeash River and the Auriol Range. This is a possible turnaround.

If continuing, follow the trail for another km or so to another marked junction. Stay on the trail to your right and loop back to the first trail junction. Follow this back to the bridge or take a left and follow a spur trail back to the RV campground and, across the road, the Park Centre.

Hike 3: Alsek Road. Medium. Up to 58 km and 3 days return.

NOTE: Most people only walk a short section of this road. Make plenty of noise, especially if biking, to let the bears know where you are. The Alsek Road is found by driving north of Haines Junction on the Alaska Highway for 10 km. The road begins on the left side of the highway across from Mackintosh Lodge. Depending on road conditions and water levels, this increasingly rough road can be driven to the first or second creek. Please park on the side of the road.

Follow on foot, or better yet, on bike as the road penetrates the valley and views open up. This road passes a large wash-out (see Hike 4), numerous creeks and horse camps until it terminates at an abandoned cabin near Sungden (a.k.a. Fergusen) Creek about 29 km from the highway. Overnight travelers will need to register at the Park Centre in Haines Junction.

Hike 4: Thunderegg Creek. Medium. Up to 4 km, and 2 hours return.

Follow instructions for the previous hike to the road junction at the second creek. Follow this obscure road or the creek bed up to the right of the washout. I can't divulge the location of the 'thundereggs' (round concentrations of inorganic material) but a keen eye may discover them. **NOTE:** Make a good mental note of the trailhead as it can be tricky to relocate.

Hike 5: Spruce Beetle Trail. Easy. 1.5 km, and up to 1 hour loop.

Drive north on the Alaska Highway for 18 km from Haines Junction. The marked trailhead is on the left; the trail begins near the outhouses. This excellent interpreted loop leads through a flower-filled forest. Halfway in, a comfortable viewing station is reached with views of Mount Archibald (the one straight ahead with the big glacier) and Mount Decoeli (the steep pinnacle on the far right).

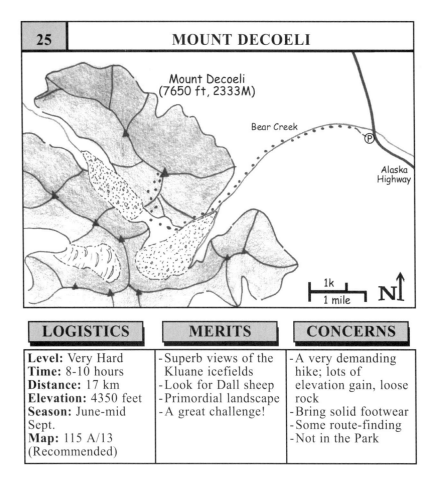

25 | MOUNT DECOELI

Mount Decoeli
(7650 ft, 2333M)

Bear Creek

Alaska
Highway

1k
1 mile

N

LOGISTICS	MERITS	CONCERNS
Level: Very Hard **Time:** 8-10 hours **Distance:** 17 km **Elevation:** 4350 feet **Season:** June-mid Sept. **Map:** 115 A/13 (Recommended)	- Superb views of the Kluane icefields - Look for Dall sheep - Primordial landscape - A great challenge!	- A very demanding hike; lots of elevation gain, loose rock - Bring solid footwear - Some route-finding - Not in the Park

From Haines Junction drive north on the Alaska Highway for 20 km. The road climbs steeply. Look for an unmarked parking area to your left immediately before the Bear Creek summit which is signposted.

Pick up an old road at the far end of the parking area. Less than 1 km later you'll reach a creek. **NOTE:** Make a note of this junction as it can be hard to find on the way out. Follow the creek for about 4 km until you reach the toe of a moraine where the drainage forks. Follow the right fork as it begins to ascend quite steadily. A steep drainage and path to your right will appear; keep left.

Continue to follow the side of the moraine for another ½ km while arcing around to a classic saddle. Ascend this pass and consider having a rest stop here before climbing the formidable-looking talus slope to the east. Decoeli's summit is no easy prize as it can take up to 2 hours to scramble up. Be aware of loose rock as you pick your way upwards to

- 112 -

the summit which is unfortunately marred by communications equipment. Return by the same route from the summit.

Option: Kimberly Meadows. Very Hard. 4-5 days and 56 km partial loop.
It is possible to do a loop to the Alsek Road (previous page) from the Mount Decoeli hike. This option is very challenging. Inquire at the Park Headquarters for more information on this route.

View Explained: If you are fortunate enough to be reading this on a clear day from the summit of Mount Decoeli, the shimmering peaks of the icefield range invite interpretation. Take out your compass and find north. Don't worry about magnetic declination for this description.
Looking about 6 km south one can see the ice-covered summit of Mount Archibald, a popular peak for beginner mountaineers.
Mount Logan, situated over 100 km away, can be seen at 250 degrees.

Due to its distance it is barely discernible. Far more visible and aesthetic is the 'Ice Palace' found at 230 degrees. Known as the Kennedy/Alverstone/Hubbard massif it simply glimmers on a sunny day.
For more details of this incredible area, consider picking up the government issue 1:250,000 maps 115B/C & 115G/F. These maps covers most of the icefields that lie within the Park.

Spring ascent of Mount Decoeli.

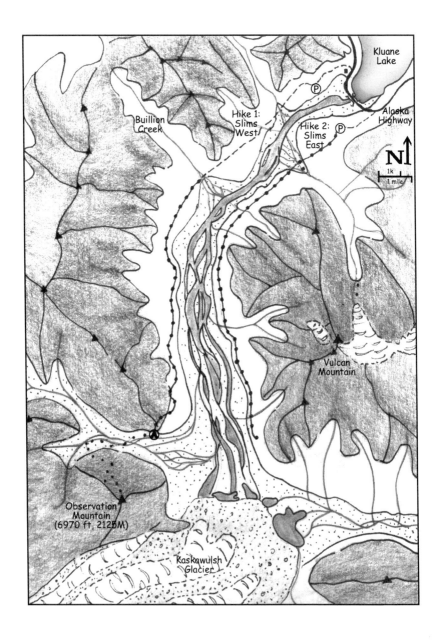

LOGISTICS	MERITS	CONCERNS

Level: Medium/ Hard
Time: 3-5 days
Distance: Up to 60km
Elev. gain: 3900 feet
(Observation Mtn.)
Season: June-Sept.
Map: 115 G/2, 115
B/15 (Useful)
	- Outstanding views of
	  the mighty
	  Kaskawulsh Glacier
	- Fascinating terrain
	- Watch for wildlife
	- Beautiful valley
	- Great views into
	  Park
		- Be VERY bear
		  aware
		- Beware of
		  'quickmud'
		- Strong winds; dusty
		- Creek crossings
		- Some route-finding
		- Trails can be vague
		-Intense creek cross
		  ings

Hike 1: Slims West. Hard. 3-5 days, and up to 60 km return.

Drive north past the Sheep Mountain Interpretive Centre, found on the shores of Kluane Lake, to the first road on your left. Follow this rough road for 2.5 km to a parking area and warden cabin.

From the parking lot the walking is easy as the old road passes around the base of Sheep Mountain, past a junction (see page 118) and to Sheep Creek 2 km in. This can be a river early in the season, a gentle creek by August. After the crossing look for a post that reconnects you with the mining road. Once again the walking is easy through poplar forests and past another junction (see page 118). A swampy area will have to be passed through before the road is picked up again.

The next major obstacle is the potentially nasty Bullion Creek almost 6 km in (see page 42 for crossing tips). If the water level is high consider following the creek down and crossing at a braided section. Look for posts upstream to reconnect to the route. The trail here is vague, or non-existent, but gets better near the bluffs and the emerging forest upstream.

The next stretch of trail has been recently improved and can be fun and swift travel. Look for cairns and posts to help stay on course. Some wet sections and some splendid dunes will be passed. Special respect must be given to the many pools of slorpy silt sludge found en route.

As you continue along the riverfront the trail begins to cross some rocky creek beds. Shortly after it dips up and into the forest; elevation gains become longer and higher with good views of the very braided Slims River.

The final 3 km of trail is the steepest stretch. A simple and cozy camp with several tent sites, fire pits and an outhouse/ bear cache is found at km 22.5. Return from here or climb Observation Mountain (next page).

Option: Observation Mountain. NOTE: This can be a long and demanding day hike. Bring lots of food, warm clothes and be prepared for an ascent of up to 3900 feet.

From the campground follow the washout up (west) along the forest-line. Look to where the washout closes together, a wide canyon. Aim 1 km below it where the river braids. Once over the creek, ascend the grassy knoll (the far side of the canyon) to the left of the creek/river. Follow it along to where it dips down and soon meets a cottongrass meadow. A footpath can be found and followed to the junction with Columbia Creek which enters from the left. The trail is vague here, look for cairns. Just under a ½ km up the trail passes close to the mountain and ends at a cliff bank. Look for a rock cairn here. The trail can be seen rising abruptly up a steep semi-vegetated slope. Don't forget to fill up the water bottle before ascending. **NOTE:** This steep trail is a much better option than routes explored further up the creek.

Follow the trail up steeply, through a subalpine area to the start of a plateau-like area. Continue in the same direction to a viewpoint or push on to the summit by following ridge systems to the east.

The summit is marked by a rock cairn. Unfortunately it's hard to make a loop of this hike (very steep and wet ravines) so returning by the same route is recommended.

The mighty Kaskawulsh Glacier.

Hike 2: Slims East. Hard. 2-4 days, and 38 km return.

From the Sheep Mountain Centre drive south on the Alaska Highway for about 3 km; the access road is marked by a parks sign. Turn right onto a rough road and follow it, if possible, for 3.5 km and park here.

From the parking area/ end of the road look for posts, cairns and markings on trees to help you cross the wide alluvial fan (Vulcan Creek). Parallel the river but stay well above it as the quickmud found near the river is a force to be reckoned with. Pick up the route/ trail at the far side of the creek as it enters into a forested area. Posts and cairns may be tricky to find. Continue down the valley, through more wet meadows and another smaller washout area.

The trail/ route then starts to follow closer to the river. The Kaskawulsh glacier comes into view about 10 km in and soon after a small lake is reached. A larger lake is found a further 5 km up the valley.

Good camping can be found near the end of the route, about 20 km up the valley. There are a number of viewpoints on the last section of trail that can be reached by some challenging bushwacking and scrambling.

Consider a trip up a drainage (creekbed) or the peak on the far end of the valley.

Dall sheep can be spotted on Sheep Mountain near the start of the Slims West hike. This mountain is an ideal habitat for the only North American sheep that stays white year round. The steep crags of Sheep Mountain provide good escape routes from predators and relatively safe lambing grounds. Loess, a type of glacier flour, blows onto the slopes and is an excellent fertilizer for the vegetation the sheep enjoy. In addition a salt lick nearby provides much-needed minerals for the beasts.

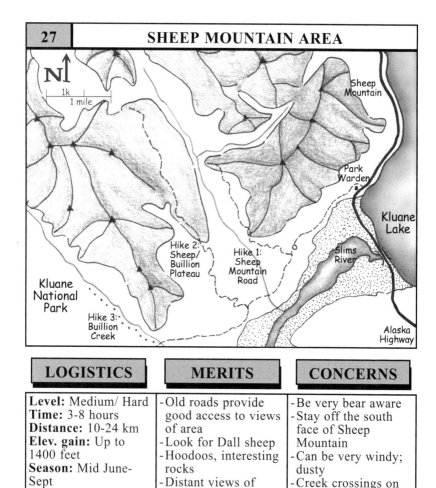

LOGISTICS	MERITS	CONCERNS
Level: Medium/ Hard **Time:** 3-8 hours **Distance:** 10-24 km **Elev. gain:** Up to 1400 feet **Season:** Mid June-Sept **Map:** 115 G/2, 115 B/15 (Useful)	-Old roads provide good access to views of area -Look for Dall sheep -Hoodoos, interesting rocks -Distant views of Kaskawulsh glacier	-Be very bear aware -Stay off the south face of Sheep Mountain -Can be very windy; dusty -Creek crossings on hikes 2 and 3

From Haines Junction drive 53 km north on the Alaska Highway to the Sheep Mountain Interpretive Centre. Continue just past the Centre and take the first left. The trailhead can be reached by walking, biking, or driving for 2.5 km along this rough gravel road. There is parking, an outhouse, and a warden cabin here.

<u>Hike 1: Sheep Creek Road.</u> Medium. 10 km and 3-4 hours return.

From the parking area pick up the road which is closed to vehicular travel. Follow it for ½ km to the first junction and take a right here. The road begins to ascend, offering excellent views a short way up. There is a total elevation gain of 1400 feet on this hike with continually improving views. Several trail junctions are encountered, stay right.

Those wishing to visit Sheep Mountain Ridge should look for a vague trail to your right just after the hoodoos (see option). For those continuing on, the 5 km signpost is a good turn-around point.

Option: Sheep Mountain Ridge.   Hard. Add 3-4 km and 2-3 hours return to first hike.

This vague trail soon peters out and you're on your own to find your way. Fortunately, the choices are fairly obvious. The steep slog to the summit ridge takes about one hour to complete. From here, one can explore the ridge, being careful to avoid crowding the sheep. NOTE: Do not descend on the south face of the mountain, return by the same route or follow the ridge out to the highway.

Hike 2: Sheep/ Bullion Plateau.   Medium/ Hard. Up to 24 km, 7-8 hours return and an elevation gain of 2900 feet.

Follow instructions for the first hike, except stay left at the first junction. Cross Sheep Creek 2 km in; this may be tricky in high water. Take a right at the second junction about 1 km further. This old road ascends steadily through the forest and eventually to an open and inviting plateau with sweeping views. Stay right at the 9.3 km post and follow the trail for another 2.5 km, along the side of the mountain and then on to a splendid alpine meadow.

Return the same way or follow a rough spur road to your right just before the end of the trail. It drops down to Sheep Creek and can be followed back to the trailhead, but it is a long walk that requires creek crossing and route-finding.

Hike 3: Bullion Creek.   Medium/ Hard. Up to 16 km and 5-6 hour return.

Follow instructions for the first hike, but stay on the main road past the first two marked junctions. Sheep Creek must be crossed 2 km in; this may be tricky in high water. Turn right at Bullion Creek almost 6 km in. Follow along the creek, if water levels permit, for several km until the ruins of an old mining camp can be seen on the far side of the creek. Cross the creek to check out (but please do not disturb) the fascinating artifacts found here. Return by the same route.

NOTE: If the water levels are too high, consider gaining some elevation along the ridges on the near side of the creek for good views of the valley and glacier.

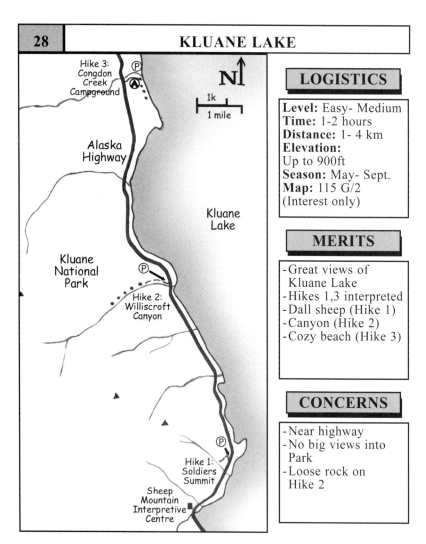

LOGISTICS

Level: Easy- Medium
Time: 1-2 hours
Distance: 1- 4 km
Elevation:
Up to 900ft
Season: May- Sept.
Map: 115 G/2
(Interest only)

MERITS

-Great views of
 Kluane Lake
-Hikes 1,3 interpreted
-Dall sheep (Hike 1)
-Canyon (Hike 2)
-Cozy beach (Hike 3)

CONCERNS

-Near highway
-No big views into
 Park
-Loose rock on
 Hike 2

Hike 1: Soldiers Summit.   Easy. ½ km and up to ½ hour return.

The marked trailhead is found on the left side of the Alaska Highway a little less than 2 km north of the Sheep Mountain Park Centre.

First off, grab the binoculars and try to spy some dall sheep that favour the crags of this mountain. Next follow the old road up as it climbs for 300 feet past some interesting historical interpretive displays about the construction of the Alaska Highway. This easy trail ends at a viewpoint overlooking Kluane Lake.

Hike 2: Williscroft Canyon.   Medium. 4 km and 1-2 hours return.

The trailhead is found on the left side of the Alaska Highway just over 8 km north of the Sheep Mountain Park Centre. Look for a green highway sign and park on the far side of the creek.

Follow the right (north) side of the creek up toward the canyon. This rough road turns into a footpath and passes numerous colorful patches of dwarf fireweed. A rock cairn partway up marks a spur trail to a good viewpoint. This is a steep and somewhat vague ascent, but enjoyable nonetheless with good views.

To travel into the canyon, simply follow the creek bed up. An obscured waterfall marks the farthest point accessible by foot. Be aware of falling rock in this area. Return by the same route.

Hike 3: Congdon Creek Campground Walk.   Easy. 1 km and ½ hour return.

The Congdon Creek Campground is found on the lake side of the Alaska Highway 16.5 km north of the Sheep Mountain Park Centre. Follow the campground road down to the waterfront. Pick up the marked trailhead to your right. This short trail leads past some interpretive signs to a viewing station. Loop back along the beachfront or continue along the lakefront where some interesting rocks and driftwood can be found.

View from Williscroft Canyon spur trail.

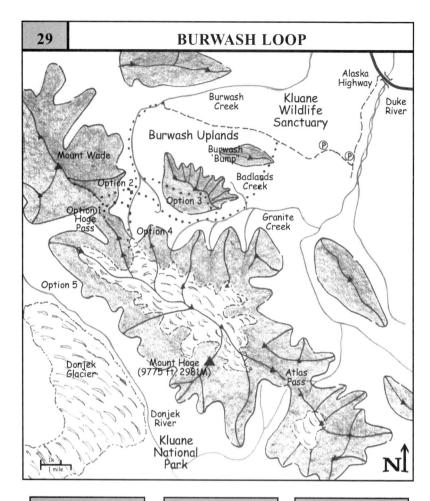

LOGISTICS

Level: Hard
Time: 3-6 days
Distance: 46 km
Elev. gain: 2500 feet
Season: June - Sept.
Map: 115 G/6
(Highly
Recommended)
-115 G/5 for Option
1, 2

MERITS

- Unique wilderness
  area; outstanding
  views
- Lots of wildlife;
  bring binoculars
- Many options from
  'basecamp'
- A true adventure !

CONCERNS

- Registration
  Mandatory
- Route-finding skills
- Be very bear aware
- Difficult terrain:
  creek crossings, wet
  tundra
- Roads marked on
  "Topo" map are
  dated, don't show all
  roads
- Give space to beasts

From Burwash Landing drive 9 km north on the Alaska Highway. Cross the Duke River and take the first left. Take an immediate right and follow this older road for 5 km, up and down a few steep sections to an abandoned camp to your right. Park here, or if your vehicle is reliable and the road isn't too wet, continue up the steep road to your right for another 1.5 km. Park by another abandoned camp.

Section 1) Burwash Creek to Lion's Paws Basecamp. Hard. 1-2 days, 25 km and 10-12 hours one way.

Start walking on the main road. Ignore a vaguer road to the right that leads upward. Follow it up for several km as views improve dramatically. Mount Hoge is the ice-walled mountain to the south; Burwash Uplands is both the plateau and the big green bump in front of Hoge. Amphitheatre Mountain, seen later, is castle-like with steep volcanic rock towers.

The road passes a number of swampy lakes as it grows vaguer. About 12 km in a reclaimed road cuts to the left across the tundra. The road is marked by several lage cut logs and makes for a good rest stop. Ignore the spur and continue on the overgrown 'cat road' (rough access road) for several more km. You will pass a small rock cairn on your left before the trail begins to descend.

(**NOTE:** This cairn marks the start of an arduous trek across wet and buggy tundra. This route, which requires a route-finding eye, can save several hours of travel time, but can be downright miserable. It is, however, a possible option if the canyons below prove impassable. If taking this option, aim for a low grassy saddle off the west side of Amphitheatre Mountain.)

Look for an old culvert in a creek bed past the cairn and start to descend. The trail can be hard to follow. Search for an old mining camp found on the far side of Burwash Creek. If you can't see the camp you may be lost; consider backtracking and trying the option mentioned above.

The first 3 km of this creek and canyon walk can be quite trying, but it's worth the effort. The creek may have to be crossed a number of times and some tricky scrambling may be required in the canyon. Consider looking for sections of an old road and game trails higher up on the south side of the creek if water levels are high.

Once through the canyon the travel becomes easier as elevation is slowly gained. The walk up the creek is lengthy but quite enjoyable. Look for two giant wooden tripods on either side of the creek; these mark the park boundary. Past here a permit is required for overnight camping.

Soon the amazing Lion's Paws hoodoos and, further on, the Burwash Glacier, appear. Look for camping near fresh water creeks.

This general area can serve as a basecamp for further exploration into the area. Please keep a clean camp! See Options 1-4.

Section 2) Lions Paws Basecamp to Trailhead. Hard. 21 km and 8-10 hours one way.

NOTE: This route out makes for a good loop and takes less time than following Burwash Creek back out. However, the bushwhack through the wet and uneven tundra/bog can be quite exhausting, so be fore-warned.

From Burwash Creek, near the hoodoos, drop down south towards the park boundary. Follow a branch of the creek on your right up and over an indistinct grassy pass to the east. Follow the pass down to Granite Creek, and then on to the appropriately-named Badlands Creek, about 4 km. Travel up Badlands Creek for less than 500 metres looking keenly for a sparsely vegetated route up. Once up, (about 20 minutes), look for a grassy saddle to the northeast about ½ km away.

Try to stay a little high and out of the backbrush. Cross to the top of saddle, marked by a pond, and sidehill over to the right. The big, green 'Burwash bump' will be in view, to the north. Aim for a low section of it and work your way down and over a creek. Ascend several hundred feet up the bump and look for two lakes once over the top. The road, if not already visible, can be picked up by passing between these lakes. From here, simply follow the road, the wonderful road, out to the trail-head.

Looking north from Hoge Pass

Option 1: Hoge Pass Viewpoint. Medium. 8 km and 2-3 hours return. NOTE: Please give the sheep in this area ample room, it's their home "24/7". Follow Burwash Creek past the warden cabin (on your right) and towards the Burwash Glacier. Look for a very rough old road on the right of the valley (the second creek), about ½ km from the cabin. Pick it up and follow it along the creek bed. Ignore any creeks that enter it as you work your way up to a wet, grassy saddle that is Hoge Pass.

Budget time in for some of the excellent ridgewalks in the area. Consider the packed scree ridge,"Cow Paddy Hill", due south. It leads up to (weather permitting) expansive views of some of Kluane's, and Canada's, highest peaks.

High camp on the flanks of Amphitheatre Mountain.

Option 2: Wade Mountain Ridgewalk. Hard. Up to 14 km, and 3-8 hours return.

Pick up the creek bed immediately to the right of the wardens cabin. It is a steep, loose and rocky ascent that could take up to an hour. Ignore a creek that comes in to the left. Once on top of a sloped plateau, walk to the edge (south) and then follow it westward. Views continue to improve and the walking is generally great with a few muddy sections. A few drops and gains of elevation are needed to reach a rocky lookout where parts of the Donjek Glacier snout can be seen. This is a good destination for a full day hike. Those wishing to attempt the summit of Mount Wade may have to budget in more time.

Option 3: Amphitheatre Mountain/ Badlands Creek.   Medium to Hard. Up to 12 km, 6 hours return, and an elevation gain of 1100 feet.

From Burwash Creek the green hill to the northeast is Amphitheatre Mountain, a truly two-faced mountain. On the south side, the walking is good on the lumpy sod and fairly moderate. On the north face, steep rocky cliffs plummet down to the depths below.

A steady 2 hour grunt across the tundra to the summit ridge is well rewarded by superb views. Several enormous peaks (Steele, Walsh) come into view to the south. The steep faces of Amphitheatre Mountain and the eroded turrets of Badlands Creek have both a rugged and sculpted character. Return by same route or loop down to Granite Creek and over the grassy saddle back to Burwash Creek.

Option 4: Burwash Glacier.   Very Hard. Up to 10 km and 4-8 hours return.

This route follows the Burwash Creek to its source at the snout of the glacier and further. Less than 1 km past the warden's cabin a sheer canyon, "the notch", will have to be passed through. Unfortunately, the creek has the same idea. Cross with caution and follow the creek up. One or two more tricky crossings may be needed before the creek flows under a massive icebridge. **NOTE:** Be aware of loose and falling rock in this area.

Hike up around to the right of the icebridge and sidehill to the snout of the glacier. Follow a creekbed to the right of the ice until the glacier's headwall comes into view. This is a good turnaround point.

Experienced mountain travelers may wish to continue up to a small pass and a possible ascent of a Mount Hoge sub-peak. Study the maps, use caution and let me know what it's like up there if you can. White-out conditions shut down my attempt in the summer of 1999.

Option 5: Donjek Glacier Loop.   Very Hard. Up to 90 km, and 6-10 days partial loop.

This is a classic trek in Kluane Park. I've bypassed this lengthy hike due to the sheer logistics (and pack weight!) of such an expedition. The idea of grunting a massive load down two steep mountain passes, and over countless creek and river crossings and through a favoured bear habitat doesn't appeal to me. Call me crazy... (or sensible if you wish.) Parks Canada has good information about this route if you want to give it a try.

CHAPTER 5

CENTRAL
AND NORTHERN YUKON

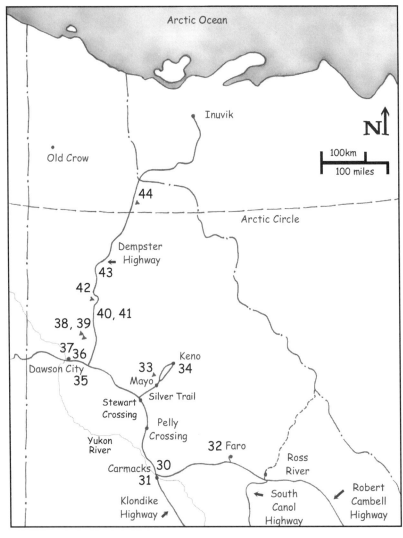

30 Carmacks Walks	36 Dawson City Walks	42 Mount Distincta
31 Agate/ Gem Trails	37 Midnight Dome	43 Sapper Hill
32 Faro Hikes	38 Monolith Viewpoint	44 Arctic Circle
33 Mount Haldane	39 Tombstone Pass	
34 Keno City Trails	40 Blueberry Hill	
35 Ridge Road	41 North Fork Pass	

The Land: This diverse region spans from the high plateaus of the interior, which includes Dawson City (home of the Klondike), to the vast treeless country above the Arctic Circle. This land is the traditional and current home of the Han, Gw'ichin, Kaska and Tutchone.

Carmacks has a unique topography of bald, rolling hills. Fireweed explodes in the numerous burn-sites of recent years. Smaller communities to the east of the Klondike Highway (Faro, Mayo, Keno) offer a more intimate look at the Yukon.

Dawson City is a must for gold rush fans and for those wanting to get into the summer vibe. Like New York City, this place doesn't sleep in the brief, mad summer.

The Dempster Highway is the only public road in North America that crosses the Arctic Circle. Harsh and beautiful, this country could be described as 'Tolkien-esque'. Near the Arctic Circle the trees disappear only to be seen in small sheltered areas. This is the true arctic, as the sharp northern wind will often remind you. Finally, Inuvik is found nestled into a strand of the mighty Mackenzie River. Here the sun shines brightly all night long during the all-to-brief summer.

Walks and Hikes: Starting in Carmacks, numerous short and easy trails give access to lakes, viewpoints and mineral deposits. Communities like Faro, Mayo, and Keno offer old

mining roads that lead to expansive vistas.

In Dawson City some fun and unofficial trails are found within the town limits. The new Ridge Road Heritage Trail, just out of Dawson, offers a historical multi-day trip overlooking the historic Klondike goldfields and the distant Ogilvie Mountain Range.

Ed Vos

The Dempster Highway has few trails but much potential for ridge walking in the Ogilvie and Richardson Ranges. It can be a harsh environment (rain, bugs, wind) and puts the wild back in wilderness. This fragile region calls for low-impact travel and camping. Wildlife sightings can be excellent along this rough stretch of road. Finally, Inuvik, a true arctic town, has a variety of easy strolls.

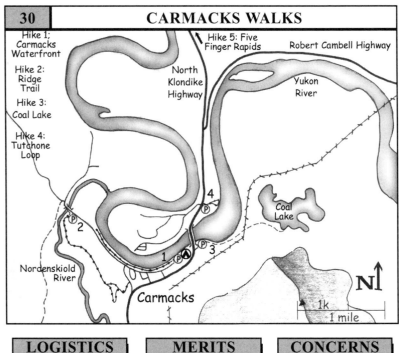

LOGISTICS	MERITS	CONCERNS

Level: Easy-Medium
Time: Up to 2 hours
Distance: Up to 6 km
Elev gain: Up to 100ft
Season: May - Sept.
Map:115 I/ 1 (Interest only)
	- Short, easy walks
	- Interpretive signs on
	  Hikes 1 and 5
	- Nice break from
	  highway driving
	- Swimming (Hike 3)
		- Hike #2 is not main
		  tained
		- Few options for con
		  tinuing hikes
		- Secure belongings if
		  staying at campsite

Hike 1: Carmacks Waterfront Boardwalk. Easy. Up to 3 km and 1 hour return.

From the gas stations in Carmacks drive or walk to the waterfront. Turn right and walk or drive to the Visitor Centre. The wheelchair accessible boardwalk follows the Yukon River past numerous interpretive panels and a number of benches for resting and watching the river flow. This trail, which occasionally crosses the road, can be followed for any desirable distance or added onto the next hike.

Hike 2: Ridge Trail. Medium. 3 km and 1 hour partial loop.

Drive or walk to the waterfront. Head left and follow it to the historic Roadhouse, found on your left just before the Nordenskiold River bridge. The unmaintained and unmarked trail can be picked up in the corner of the lawn behind the roadhouse.

The foot path follows the river upstream and then begins to gain in elevation. Views are good as the trail slowly loops back to Carmacks. Trails braid in some sections but generally lead in the same direction. Stay high until near the highway. Drop down on the trail past the First Nations grave markers (small coloured houses). These are not a tourist attraction; please do not disturb or photograph. Work your way back into town from here.

Hike 3: Coal Lake.   Medium. 4 km and 1-2 hours return.

If driving north, the marked trailhead is found just before the Yukon River bridge, on your right. Park by the sign and pick up the trail which starts down the road and along the Yukon River. This old road/foot-trail follows the banks of the Yukon River, past some mining relics and then over or around a small, steep trail section. The trail then veers into the forest and eventually to Coal Lake. The waters simply glimmer on a sunny day. Good for swimming, picnicking etc.

Hike 4: Northern Tutchone Loop.   Easy. 1 km and ½ hour loop.

This trail can be found behind the Northern Tutchone Visitor Centre. The centre, well worth a visit, is located just across the Yukon River bridge, to your right, on the way north out of Carmacks.

This easy loop cuts through the forest and past numerous First Nations' shelters. Stay left at first trail junction. The trail meets the Yukon River where there is a bench for resting. From the bench follow the trail to the right (upriver) and pick up the other side of the loop (first right) which then leads back to the trailhead.

Hike 5: Five Finger Rapids.   Medium. 0.5 km and up to 0.5 hour return.

Drive out of Carmacks for 23 km along the Klondike Highway. The marked trailhead is on your left.

A long series of stairs drops down to a number of interpretive panels, and a viewing area of the infamous rapids which were a major impediment to sternwheeler and stampeder traffic during the heady days of the Klondike gold rush.

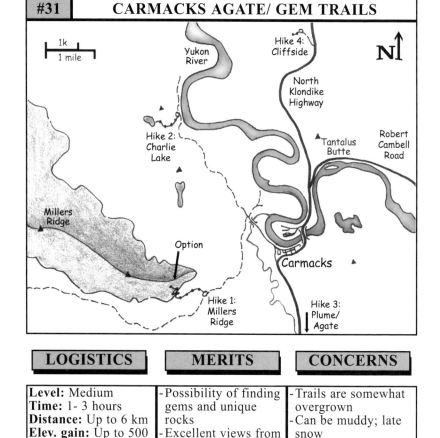

LOGISTICS	**MERITS**	**CONCERNS**
Level: Medium **Time:** 1- 3 hours **Distance:** Up to 6 km **Elev. gain:** Up to 500 feet **Season:** June - Sept. **Map:**115 I/ 1 (Interest only)	-Possibility of finding gems and unique rocks -Excellent views from first hike -Diverse forests, berries and mush rooms	-Trails are somewhat overgrown -Can be muddy; late snow -Rough roads en-route to trail-heads

Hike 1: Millers Ridge: Medium. 4 km and 2-3 hours return.

NOTE: This is the finest of the Agate trails; highly recommended. Drive to the Carmacks riverfront. Take a left and follow the road past the Roadhouse and over the Nordenskiold River bridge. Head left onto the Nansen Creek Road. Follow this rough road for 4 km; the marked trailhead is on your right. Pick up the footpath to the left of the sign. Follow this rough footpath through a lush and often wet forest until it starts to gain elevation. Some interesting green speckled rocks can be found about two-thirds of the way in. Views improve as the trail switchbacks steeply upwards and ends abruptly at a loose, rocky sub-peak. Return by the same way, or consider the Option.

Option: Millers Ridgewalk. Very Hard. Add 1 km and 1-2 hours return.

Consider a trip to the top of the bluffs, a hearty workout. (Beware of loose rock in this area.) From the top of the trail (Hike 1) drop down until you have a view of an open area below the crags. Work your way through the brush and onto the slope. An ascent of the loose, steep scree run can be quite strenuous. A thrilling ridge walk with expansive views and fascinating rock sculptures is the reward for your toil.

Hike 2: Charlie Lake.   Medium. 5 km and 2 hours return.

From the highway, near the gas stations, take any road down to the river. Take a left, drive over the Nordenskiold River, and stay straight on the rough Freegold Road. Look for a trail sign in the bush to your left, just under 6 km from the bridge. There is a small pullover just before the sign, marked by several bright red/orange poles.

The trail begins by the sign as an ATV road but soon becomes a fairly overgrown single-track trail. A few rock towers and cliffs are passed which presumably contain the mysterious agates. The forest is diverse, with some pure stands of northern trees, berries, wildflowers, and mushrooms to delight the senses. The trail soon crosses and follows a small creek (avoid the temptation to drink this water) up and down to a small swampy lake. There is some moderate potential from here for cruising around.

Hike 3: Plume Agate and Mineral Trail.   Medium. 3 km and 1 hour return.

This rough and poorly maintained trail can be found on the right side of the highway 14 km (km marker 344) south of Carmacks. Two attempts by the author at walking it resulted in wet feet as a creek seems to have taken over the trail. Not recommended for a long hike, but the berries and wildflowers may interest some people.

Hike 4: Cliffside.   Medium. 100 feet and 5 minutes return.

This isn't much of a trail, but it makes for a pleasant picnic and rock hounding stop.

Just over 4.5 km north of the Carmacks city limits a trail sign can barely be seen to the left. Follow this rough road for just over 1 km to an obviously marked trail sign. A footpath can be picked up just past the sign. A short, steep trail leads to good views of the Carmacks area valley.

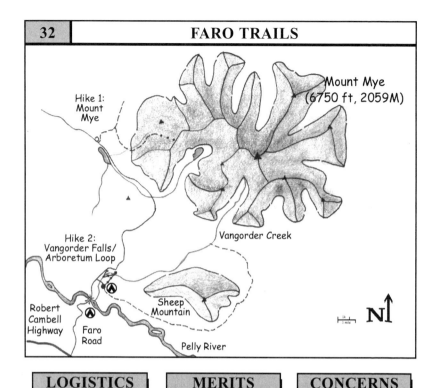

LOGISTICS	**MERITS**	**CONCERNS**
Level: Medium **Time:** 2- 4 hours **Distance:** 3- 12 km **Elev. gain:** Up to 2400 feet (Hike 1) **Season:** June - Sept. **Map:** 105 K/6 (Recommended for option)	- Good access to beautiful high country with great views; lots of room to roam (Hike 1) - Watch for wildlife - Waterfall (Hike 2)	- Please don't crowd wildlife - Some mining garbage (Hike 1) - Can be wet; boggy - May encounter motorized traffic

Hike 1: Mount Mye Highlands. Medium. 3-4 hours and up to 12 km return.

From the town of Faro turn right onto the Mine Road and follow it for 16 km. Watch for a steep, narrow ATV (All Terrain Vehicle) road on your right. If the mine is operating, park about half a km down from here on your left. If the mine is not operating, consider parking on the side of this wide road just down from the (unmarked) trailhead.

After about 50 metres of going up, you will encounter a wide haul road. Cross it and pick up the trail just down to your left. This old road climbs slowly for about 2 km. Watch carefully for an even vaguer road to your right. If you pass some large oil drums and mining bric-a-brac, you've gone a bit too far.

Follow this road for about 3 km total. You will encounter a very sketchy bridge which looks very unstable. Consider dropping down to the creek to avoid this potential hazard. The trail now begins to climb fairly steadily, reaches some excellent viewpoints and eventually peters out some 2 km further. Return by same way or consider the Option.

Option: Mount Mye Plateau. Medium. Add 1-12 km and 1-4 hours.

From the end of the road the options open up for exploration. One suggestion is to continue in a north-east direction for several km to a wonderful viewing area of an unnamed subalpine lake. Numerous subpeaks in the area serve to entice the happy wanderer. Please do not crowd any wildlife that may be encountered.

Keep your bearings as the old road may be hard to pick up on the way back. Bushwhacking down to the highway is not recommended as the forest can be very dense.

Hike 2: VanGorder Falls/Arboretum Trail. Medium. 3 km and up to 2 hours return or loop.

NOTE: Those desiring an easier and shorter trail near Faro may wish to consider this recently expanded trail system.

From the Interpretive Centre in Faro cross the road and walk around the top end (go left at the junction) of the John Connelly RV campground loop. The marked trailhead can be spotted on your left.

The trail goes by numerous benches, slowly gains elevation, passes a spur trail to the Arboretum to the left and ends at a viewing station that overlooks VanGorder Falls. Return by the same route or take the (summer only) spur trail to make a partial loop to the Arboretum. From this botanical garden return by the way you came, follow the Arboretum loop or take the Faro Mine Road south (left) back to Faro.

Wildlife: Mount Mye is the home of a small but hardy herd of Fannin Sheep. Recently protected, this unique form of sheep is a hybrid of Dall and Stone Sheep, and is very rare. Seemingly oblivious to the hustle and bustle of Faroites, the sheep can be spotted during the fall to spring time from numerous viewing stations found around Mount Mye. For locations of the viewing stations, and other hiking routes in this area, visit the recently completed Cambell Region Interpretive Centre. It is well worth a visit and has some excellent displays on local wildlife and the history of the Faro area.

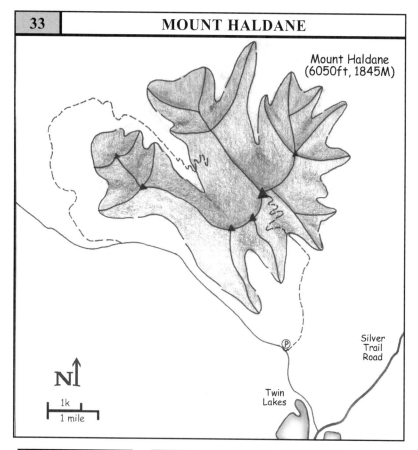

Mount Haldane
(6050ft, 1845M)

Silver
Trail
Road

N↑

1k
1 mile

Twin
Lakes

LOGISTICS	MERITS	CONCERNS
Level: Medium/ Hard **Time:** 5-7 hours **Distance:** 12 km **Elev. gain:** 3900 feet **Season:** July - Sept. **Map:** 105 M/ 13 (Useful)	-Old road provides good access; big views -Ridge walking potential -Consider visiting the lodge afterwards	-Substantial elevation gain -Some loose rock -Watch the weather near top; windy -Possible late snow

(**NOTE:** Those desiring a shorter trail in the Mayo area may wish to check out the 4 km loop around Five mile Lake. This campsite and day-use area is found a little over 6 km east of Mayo on the Silver Trail.) From the town of Mayo (50 km down the Silver Trail Highway) drive east for a little over 26 km. A resort can be seen on your right, and just past it look for a road to your left. A hard-to-spot sign marking the

Mount Haldane hike is posted there. Follow this road for 3 km to a parking area with several outhouses.

Follow on foot or bike along this old mining road, taking note of a junction with another road less than ½ km in. The road is easy going for the first several km before starting to gain in elevation. Although poor weather conditions shut down my summit attempt, a number of sources have confirmed that the trail is easy to follow. This steep gradient is now the norm as the road continues to ascend until the summit is reached some 4 km later. The trail is clearly marked the whole way up as it goes through a series of steep switchbacks. The final push to the summit is quite taxing, but in typical fashion well worth the effort. Return by same route or consider the following Option.

Option: Mount Haldane Highlands. Hard. Add 1-6 km and 1-3 hours.

Obvious ridge systems present themselves to parties prepared for a little off-trail action; a study of the map may be of assistance. A return route by the road at the back side of the mountain seems like a possible, though very lengthy, way of making a loop. If you plan on attempting this, it would be wise to have a shuttle vehicle waiting or plan an overnight trip. Apparently, the folks in Mayo plan on establishing an official trail on this road in the near future.

A rocky cairn is found on the summit of Mount Haldane and visitors are invited to leave their names in the log book found there. Rock cairns are seen on many mountain peaks throughout the territory and are useful for plane navigation. Smaller piles of rocks are occasionally found on trails and serve as helpful and relatively unobtrusive markers.

Also common further north are inukshuks (right) which were used by First Nations people for landmarks as well as being used occasionally to herd animals into traps. Seeing the likeness of a human form in the open arctic barren-grounds may have also helped relieve a sense of loneliness.

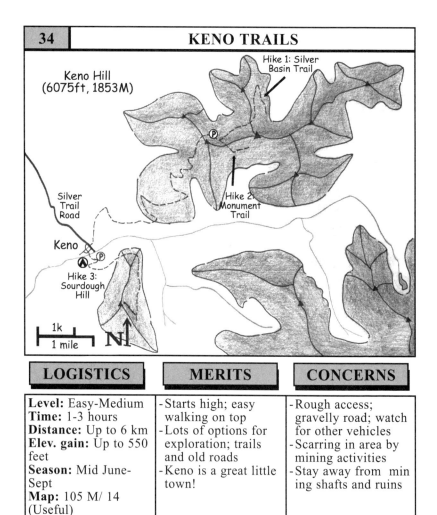

Keno Hill
(6075ft, 1853M)

Hike 1: Silver Basin Trail

Silver Trail Road

Keno

Hike 2: Monument Trail

Hike 3: Sourdough Hill

1k
1 mile

N

LOGISTICS	MERITS	CONCERNS
Level: Easy-Medium **Time:** 1-3 hours **Distance:** Up to 6 km **Elev. gain:** Up to 550 feet **Season:** Mid June-Sept **Map:** 105 M/ 14 (Useful)	- Starts high; easy walking on top - Lots of options for exploration; trails and old roads - Keno is a great little town!	- Rough access; gravelly road; watch for other vehicles - Scarring in area by mining activities - Stay away from mining shafts and ruins

Hike 1: Silver Basin Trail. Easy. 6 km and 2 hours return.

Drive to the museum in Keno, turn left and proceed a short distance to where the road splits into three sections. The middle road, which can be hiked, biked or driven, gains elevation steadily as it follows numerous switchbacks up to a parking area 10.5 km later.

From the parking area and signpost follow the marked trail system to a dilapidated cabin and trail junction. Go left and follow the old road to a good viewing area. This is a pleasant and easy high-country stroll.

Hike 2: Monument Trail. Easy. 2 km and 1 hour return.

From the trail junction listed above turn right instead of left. Follow it for about 1 km until it fades away. This old road passes near some interesting rock formations and some ruins of old mining operations. It is possible to explore further from here along the main ridge.

Hike 3: Sourdough Hill. Medium. 10 km and 2-3 hours return.

Looking at the Keno museum, take the road to the left of the front of the building. Follow the road by foot or car, past the campground and over Lightning Creek. Once across the bridge take the steep road to your right. Park around here or drive for approximately 1 km further. Caution is necessary as the road is somewhat steep and washed out.

Continue on foot up this road, ignoring smaller roads that spur off, for a total of 4 km from town.

A road branches off to the left at this point and was not marked at the time of writing. Follow it for a little over 1 km. A trail marker will be encountered on your right.

Follow this vague footpath, also marked, to a viewpoint with a rock cairn and a signpost that points out local peaks.

Other Options: There are numerous old mining roads in the Keno area. With some planning and map studying, numerous overnight hiking options or bike routes exist for the truly adventurous. Consider picking up the topographical map of the area (see previous page).

The town of Keno was created in 1919 following a rich silver and galena strike, but the mines have been closed since 1989. The signpost on Keno Hill, erected by homesick miners, is a popular photo shoot location for tourists today.

Mining in the Keno area, like many other places in the Yukon, has shut down and tourism is now the major industry. Keno is a wonderful place to visit; a real northern experience. The two dozen locals operate a café, museum and tavern as well as a nice, comfortable campground.

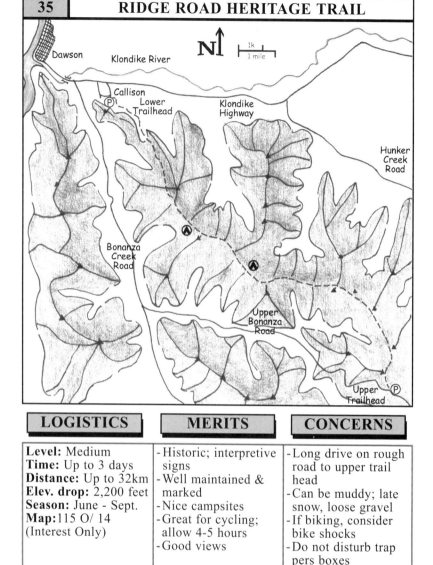

LOGISTICS	MERITS	CONCERNS
Level: Medium **Time:** Up to 3 days **Distance:** Up to 32km **Elev. drop:** 2,200 feet **Season:** June - Sept. **Map:** 115 O/ 14 (Interest Only)	- Historic; interpretive signs - Well maintained & marked - Nice campsites - Great for cycling; allow 4-5 hours - Good views	- Long drive on rough road to upper trail head - Can be muddy; late snow, loose gravel - If biking, consider bike shocks - Do not disturb trap pers boxes

NOTE: It is possible to start this hike at the lower trailhead and hike or bike a smaller portion. See Option 1. For the full distance, it's best to start at the top. Drive out of Dawson (towards Whitehorse) for a little over 2 km. Just past the Klondike River bridge and the gas station, look for the Bonanza Creek Road on your right; it is marked by a sign.

Follow this historic road for a little over 13 km. You will pass a massive gold mining dredge along the way which is worth a visit. About 1 km further, a junction with the Upper Bonanza Road is reached. Turn left and follow this even rougher road for another 12 km. The trailhead, on your left, is clearly marked by a cedar sand-blasted sign..

This historic haul road trail is clearly marked. Very pleasant campgrounds (tentsites, outhouses, picnic tables, water pumps and fire-pits) await 13 km and 20 km in from the upper trailhead. These campsites are built by former roadhouse locations. History buffs will surely enjoy the interpretive signs and gold rush era bric-a-brac found along the trail.

The lower trailhead is located in the Callison industrial area several km out of Dawson. Follow the Callison Road out to the Klondike Highway and turn left to return to Dawson. (See option 1 for more details of lower trailhead.)

Option 1: Ridge Road (Lower Section.) Medium. Time and distance variable.

From Dawson City head east on the Klondike Highway (towards Whitehorse) for 4 km. Look for the second entrance into the Callison Industrial area; it is marked by an illustrated sign of a hiker. Turn right and follow the road to the end. Go left at another hiker sign and then up a short, rough road to the trailhead which is clearly marked. The trail gains elevation for the first ten km or so with slowly emerging views. An tenting trip to the lower campground, just over 11 km in, may serve as an enjoyable overnight trip. The other campsite is 15 km in.

Option 2: King Solomon Dome/Goldfields. Medium. Time and distance variable.

Bikers may be interested in studying the maps of the area around this hike, as many old and modern roads look very inviting for two-wheel travel. King Solomon Dome (4050 feet) is the highest point in the Klondike area and can be reached easily from the upper trailhead.

The Ridge Road was constructed at the turn of the century as an efficient way of moving the goods out of the goldfields. The first Territorially-funded road, it was built on high ground to avoid the boggy valley bottoms. Above is 'Soda Station', found near the upper trailhead.

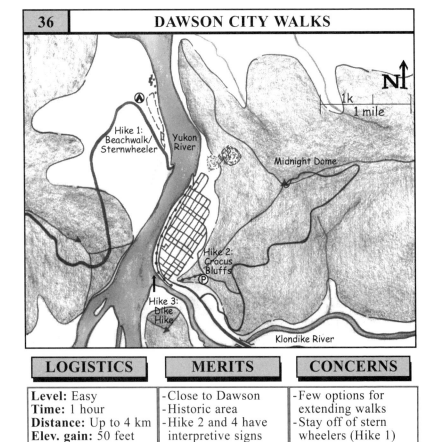

LOGISTICS	MERITS	CONCERNS

Level: Easy
Time: 1 hour
Distance: Up to 4 km
Elev. gain: 50 feet
Season: May - Sept.
Map: 116 B/ 3
(Interest only)
	- Close to Dawson
	- Historic area
	- Hike 2 and 4 have
	  interpretive signs
	- Nice beach (Hike 1)
		- Few options for
		  extending walks
		- Stay off of stern
		  wheelers (Hike 1)

Hike 1: Beachwalk/Sternwheeler Graveyard. Easy. 3 km and 1 hour return.

From Dawson hop on the ferry and cross the Yukon River. Follow the Top of the World Highway for less than ½ km to the government campground which is found on your right. Follow the lower campground road, past some interpretive displays. There is a trail near the peregrine falcon sign. Drop down to the beach and keep following it to the shipwrecks or, if the water level is high, stay on the campground road.

After a ten minute stroll this road leads away from the river. Turn right and walk down to the beach. If the water level is not too high, walk upriver for several hundred metres. What little remains of the old ships Schwatka, Seattle 3 and Julia B are found in the bush to your left. Please stay off these potentially dangerous wrecks.

Return by same route or follow the beach back as far as you can before looping back to the campground road.

Hike 2: Crocus Bluffs.   Easy. 1 km and ½ hour return.

The marked trailhead can be found by following King Street up to where it turns into the Old Dome Road (a.k.a. the Mary McCloud Road). The trailhead is found on the right less than 1 km up this steep, and sometimes slick road.

Follow this maintained trail past several interprctive panels to a good viewing station of the confluence of the Yukon and Klondike Rivers. Return by the same route or descend a steep and loose spur trail back to town. This trail can be found just down from the viewing platform.

NOTE: Rock climbers may wish to check out page 47.

Hike 3: Dike Hike.   Easy. Up to 4 km and up to 1 hour return.

The dike, built after a particularly bad spring flood in 1979, can be reached at any point near the Yukon River. Pick up the trail at Crocus Bluffs, the ferry landing or any point in-between. To do the full length, consider starting the walk across from Crocus Bluffs and following it for 2 km to the ferry landing. Return the same way or make a loop by cutting through town. Dawson has some very unique architecture which is definitely worth investigating.

Hike 4: Klondike Campground Loop.   Easy. 3 km and 1 hour loop.

This well-maintained trail is found at the government campground 17 km out of downtown Dawson. Follow the Klondike Highway out of town, and just past the airport. Take a left onto Rock Creek Road and then another left into the campground. Follow the loop to the right and

look for the hard-to-spot trailhead, also on your right. If driving to Dawson, look for the second entrance to the Rock Creek subdivision around km 507.

This interpreted loop passes through the forest, past some beaver ponds and wildflowers to the banks of the historic Klondike River. The trail loops back to the trailhead from here.

Dawson City during the goldrush.

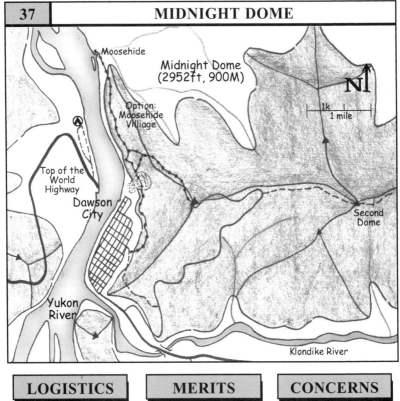

LOGISTICS	MERITS	CONCERNS
Level: Medium/ Hard **Time:** 3-4 hours return **Distance:** 6 km **Elev. gain:** 2000 feet **Season:** May-Sept **Map:**116 B/ 3 (Interest only)	- Close to town (Dawson) - Amazing views of area - Lots of options - A fun challenge	- Some loose rock and steep sections may be encountered - Inevitable meeting with RV traffic on summit - Possible late snow

The unmarked trailhead can be found by following King Street up and away from the waterfront. This road turns into the Mary Macleod Road and is known locally as the Old Dome Road. Follow it for a little over 100 metres while looking for a ditch/trail to your left. Follow the ditch for about 50 metres looking for a foot-trail on your right. This is the start of the hike. The foot-trail meets up with another foot-trail halfway to the slide; this can be used on the way back to return to Dawson. After a kilometre or so of slow elevation gain you'll reach the rockslide. Walking across is not as treacherous as it seems to be at first, but caution is necessary when travelling through the loose and shifting boulders. Look for a well-used footpath to your right, shortly after crossing the rockslide. This, and another trail to your right less than a ½ km down (marked by flagging tape), are access trails to the Dome summit; the second trail being better. Continue on the main trail for Option 1 (see below).

From here on get ready for a good cardio-vascular workout as the trail climbs steadily for about ½ km. Upon reaching the north flank of the dome, the trail evens out a bit while passing through boreal forest with emerging views of the surrounding area. Getting close to the summit, the trail begins to braid; simply continue in the same direction until the viewing area and the road are reached. Return by the same route, or follow the road down which is an easier but longer option.

View Explained: Looking southeast one can see the valley where Bonanza and Eldorado Creeks empty out. Massive tailing piles and other industrial mayhem can be seen in this area. Looking due south and to the west the mighty Yukon River can be seen as well as its confluence with the Klondike River. Dawson City sits to the west, and across the river from it, the Top of the World Highway is clearly visible.

The Yukon River continues its unstoppable course to the ocean passing Moosehide Village on river right. To the northwest and to the north and northeast the impressive Ogilvie Mountain Range invite the modern adventurer.

Partially visible to the east is the 'Second Dome'. The Second Dome Road, found a little over 1 km down the Midnight Dome Road, can be followed up to even better views of the area. This is also the start of the unofficial Klondike Pipeline Trail, see page 50.

Option: Moosehide Village. Medium. Add 8 km and 2-3 hours return to Hike 1.

NOTE: Permission to visit Moosehide must be obtained, prior to embarking on this hike, from the First Nations Band Office located at 3rd and Queen Streets. Phone: 993-5385

Follow the instructions of the previous hike, but stay on the main trail after crossing the slide. Good lookout points are encountered en route. A steep, eroded section may intimidate some folks; use extreme caution or turn back.

If you continue, the trail begins to slowly descend through the forest and a somewhat marshy section. Near the end of the hike you will reach a small bridge. Cross the bridge and go straight, ignoring several spur trails. Interesting interpretive signs are found near the old church. Please respect the residents by not straying far from the church area.

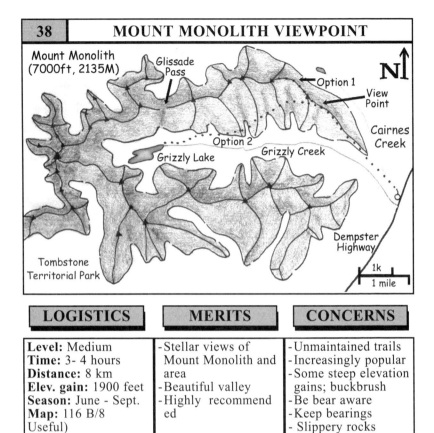

LOGISTICS	MERITS	CONCERNS

Level: Medium
Time: 3- 4 hours
Distance: 8 km
Elev. gain: 1900 feet
Season: June - Sept.
Map: 116 B/8
Useful)
	- Stellar views of
	  Mount Monolith and
	  area
	- Beautiful valley
	- Highly recommend
	  ed
		- Unmaintained trails
		- Increasingly popular
		- Some steep elevation
		  gains; buckbrush
		- Be bear aware
		- Keep bearings
		- Slippery rocks

NOTE: If planning an overnight trip registration at the Tombstone campground is recommended.

The trailhead is located 58.5 km up the Dempster Highway, or 13 km south of the Tombstone campground. Look for a large gravel pit on the west side of the road. The trail begins in the far corner of the parking area; there are often vehicles parked here. This trailhead often has garbage around, and sometimes bears. It's best not to camp here.

Follow an old road for a few hundred metres until it turns into an unofficial trail. The path is fairly level for the first several km as it passes through a pleasant forest and parallels Cairnes Creek. As the trail begins to gain in elevation, views of Monolith emerge slowly until a superb viewing area is reached about 4 km in. This is an excellent place for a lunch break. Return by the same route or consider the options.

Option 1: Grizzly Ridge. Hard. Add 1-4 km and 1-3 hours return.

From the viewing stations described above, consider climbing further up the ridge system for increasingly spectacular views of Monolith and the surrounding area. Some travelers prefer this high line to get to the lake and/or the pass. As one climbs higher, the brush begins to thin out and the ridge turns into a scree and talus route. Try to stay high on the ridge as numerous ravines cut down the side of the mountain, making travel quite tedious. Return by the same route.

Option 2: Grizzly Lake. Very Hard. Add 6 hours and 6 km to Mount Monolith Viewpoint hike.
NOTE: This calculation does not include return time; a trip to the lake and back out is an extremely long day trip and is probably best split into two or three days. A topographical map of the area (see previous page) is recommended.
From the viewing station (Hike 1) sidehill around the rocky subpeak directly ahead of you. Once around this obstacle you will want to slowly arc your way downwards, remembering to try and stay above the (evil) buckbrush and just below the scree. This 'line' can be very vague at times; however if you find yourself waist-high or (God forbid) over your head in nasty brush, you are definitely too low.
The first major ravine (drainage) you hit will be the worst and it may take some time to drop down into and rise out of. You will cross numerous other ravines en route to Grizzly Lake, but they will be passed at a lower elevation where they tend to be wider. Try to avoid hitting these drainages too high up as travel can be very inefficient.
Continue to drop slowly for several more km. Soon you may be able to pick your way along the flat but often wet valley floor. Several more km and the route roughly parallels Grizzly Creek. Several unofficial campsites can be found near close end of the lake. Please practice low-impact camping.

The Mount Monolith/Tombstone Mountain Range stands as a dramatic example of the powers of nature. This batholith was created thousands of years ago as igneous rock pushed through the layers of sedimentary rock, cooled and hardened. Over millennia the surrounding sedimentary rock eroded, exposing the sheer towers and pillars seen today.

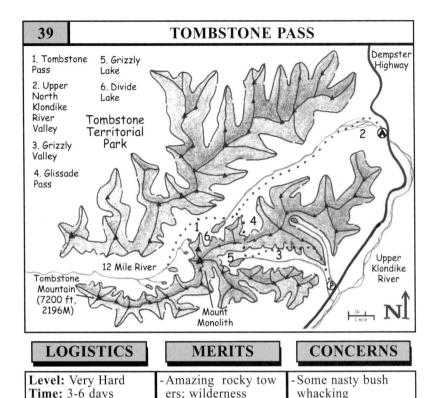

1. Tombstone Pass
2. Upper North Klondike River Valley
3. Grizzly Valley
4. Glissade Pass
5. Grizzly Lake
6. Divide Lake

Tombstone Territorial Park

Dempster Highway

Upper Klondike River

12 Mile River

Tombstone Mountain (7200 ft, 2196M)

Mount Monolith

LOGISTICS	MERITS	CONCERNS
Level: Very Hard **Time:** 3-6 days **Distance:** Up to 42 km **Elev. gain:** 2900 feet **Season:** Mid June - Sept **Maps:** 116 B/7, 116 B/8 (Recommended)	- Amazing rocky towers; wilderness - Hearty challenge for experienced back packers - Wildflowers and wildlife - A real adventure!	- Some nasty bush whacking - Can be very wet - Practice low-impact travel and camping - Tricky route-finding - Late snow - Be bear aware

NOTE: This hike starts at the end of Option 2; previous page. It is also possible to start a hike into Tombstone Pass via the Option on the following page. The Option requires less elevation gains/losses and is preferred over the Grizzly Valley approach by some hikers. Registration at the Tombstone Campground is recommended.

Glissade Pass/Divide Lake: This high rocky pass, which drops down into a steep cirque, is located due north from the east (closest) end of Grizzly Lake. **NOTE:** Steep, loose rock, late snow and a gain and loss of about 3000 feet make this traverse fairly strenuous. One option is to pack light for a long day trip over the pass and back. The climb up is a steady but reasonable grunt. Once up, look for a scree run to the west of the narrow saddle. Drop down slowly into Axeman creek below and avoid the temptation to stay too high (unless camping), as its largely impassable to the west. Follow the creek as it curves into the Upper Klondike River Valley and follow the valley up to the picturesque Divide Lake, where finding a nice, dry campsite can take a little time. Please be low impact in this pristine area.

Tombstone Pass: The trip over this pass is a treat compared to all the rocky and brushy travel encountered thus far. After a fairly substantial elevation gain the views of the Batholith become somewhat obscured for a short time. This allows anticipation to build as one begins a very gradual descent into what looks like a giant primordial amphitheatre. Views continue to improve as this outstanding area is reached. There are many options for strolling around, checking out the many small lakes, camping, flower sniffing etc. Return back to Divide Lake by the same way. From here you can go back to Grizzly Valley over Glissade Pass and out to the road, or consider the Option found below.

Option: Upper North Klondike River Valley. Very Hard. This option should take one very long day or two shorter ones. This route/trail requires some bushwacking, route-finding and a creek crossing. Some hikers prefer the high line on the south side of the valley, around 4 to 5000 feet.

Once back at Divide Lake, cross it again and proceed down the valley parallelling the river. It is generally better to try to find some higher ground a short distance from the river. It's hard to find a perfect line through the gnarled flora, but, fear not, a vague horse path can be picked up not far from the lake. It can be tricky to locate, but is worth searching for. This sketchy trail, which braids and occasionally disappears altogether, soon starts to swing closer to the river before crossing it, at a wide point, about 2 km from the highway. The trail can be picked up again once across the river, and soon joins the Tombstone Campground Interpretive trail, which leads back to the government campground.

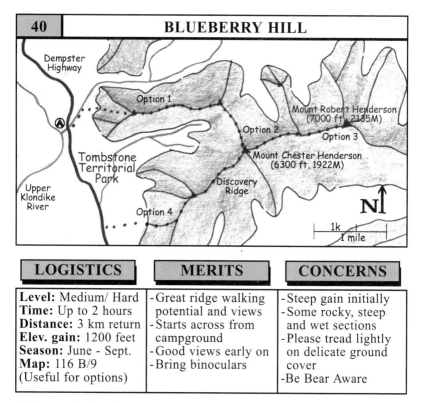

LOGISTICS

Level: Medium/ Hard
Time: Up to 2 hours
Distance: 3 km return
Elev. gain: 1200 feet
Season: June - Sept.
Map: 116 B/9
(Useful for options)

MERITS

- Great ridge walking potential and views
- Starts across from campground
- Good views early on
- Bring binoculars

CONCERNS

- Steep gain initially
- Some rocky, steep and wet sections
- Please tread lightly on delicate ground cover
- Be Bear Aware

Drive to the Tombstone campground which is located 71.5 km up the Dempster Highway. Park here.

(NOTE: Those looking for a short and easy trail near the campground may be interested in the 1 km interpreted loop which begins near the public shelter. There are some rough and overgrown sections. Free guided tours are available during the summer months; contact the good folks at the Interpretive Centre, which is also an excellent educational stop.)

Walk across the road and pick up a rough footpath on the right side of Charcoal (a.k.a. Black Shale) Creek. Take the trail that closely follows the Creek for less than ½ km until it turns to the right and continues up through a mossy hillside. The trail is very steep and muddy until a rocky promontory is reached. This is excellent for a well-deserved rest stop and is a possible turn-around point. Return the same way or consider the options listed below.

Option 1: Henderson Ridge Walk. Medium. Add up to 6 km and up to 3 hours to Blueberry Hill hike.

Continue along the obvious ridge system in an easterly direction for several km. A rocky ridge/subpeak will now be in view; continue in the same general direction. The route is straightforward and a delight to travel on. Return by the same way or consider the next option.

Option 2: Mount Chester Henderson. Hard. Add 2 km and 1-2 hours to the previous hike and Option.
It is a steep, rocky scramble up to the summit ridge of Chester Henderson. Consider Option 3 and 4 which start from here.

Option 3: Mount Robert Henderson. Very Hard. Add 5 km and 3-4 hours to the hikes described above. **NOTE:** Very long day trip.
From Chester the pinnacle-shaped peak of Mount Robert Henderson beckons to the east. Once again the route is obvious. It should take about an hour to reach the base of the rocky pyramid. A steep talus climb to the summit provides a hearty challenge and is rewarded by superb views of the Southern Ogilvies. Return by the same route.

Option 4: Discovery Ridge. Very Hard. Add 6 km and 3-4 hours to Option 2.
From the rocky summit of Mount Chester Henderson arc around in a southerly direction along a rocky ridge system. Be aware of loose rock and steep cliffs as you continue along. Finding a line back down to the highway presents some route-finding challenges. The ridge second from the last seems best. A difficult descent leads to a tricky bushwhack back to the highway. Turn right; it's a little over 2 km along the road back to the campground.

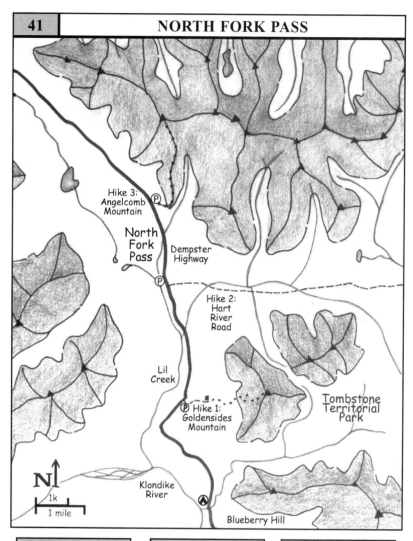

Hike 3:
Angelcomb
Mountain

North
Fork
Pass

Dempster
Highway

Hike 2:
Hart
River
Road

Lil
Creek

Hike 1:
Goldensides
Mountain

Tombstone
Territorial
Park

Klondike
River

Blueberry Hill

N

1k
1 mile

LOGISTICS	MERITS	CONCERNS
Levels: Medium-Hard **Time:** 1-8 hours **Distance:** 1-20 km **Elevation gain:** Up to 2200 feet **Season:** June to Aug **Map:** 116 B/9 (Useful)	-Open area with beautiful tundra valleys -Rock towers; -Many options -Ridge walking -Look for Dall sheep, Caribou - Hikes start at high elevations	-Area can be muddy, wet, late snow -Can be buggy -Please tread lightly on ground cover -Keep bearings - Don't crowd wildlife

Hike 1: Goldensides Mountain. Medium/Hard. 4 km, 3-4 hours return and 2000 foot elevation gain.

From the Tombstone campground (71.5 km up the Dempster Highway) walk or drive 4 km north. Turn right onto a short, steep road which leads to a small equipment station and the start of the hike. If driving, please park unobtrusively by the side of the entrance to this road.

Rough trails can be picked up from the transmitter tower further up the road and followed towards the mountain. From the base it is a fairly steady elevation gain. The trails disappear so you will have to find a route up. It may be helpful to try doing a traverse line (zigzagging your way up). Upon reaching the summit area, numerous rest spots are present, and this high ground can be interesting, although limited, to explore. Return by the same route.

View Explained: From the summit of Goldensides Mountain look for the following features on a clear day.

The most obvious landmark is the steep spire of Tombstone Mountain, to the west up the Upper Klondike River Valley. Mount Monolith is partially visible to the left of Tombstone. To the north lies the Hart River Valley (see below).The peak closest to Goldensides is named Blackcap Mountain. To the south and south east lies the massive ridge system of Mount Chester/ Robert Henderson, Hike # 40, previous page.

Hike 2: Hart River Road. Medium. 1-20 km and 1-8 hours return.

NOTE: This old road can be very muddy and is best tried in August or September. Not for motorized vehicles.

From the Tombstone campground (71.5 km up the Dempster Highway) drive or bike north for 7 km. Hart River Road is on your right; a small parking area is found about 20 metres further up the road on your left.

This rough road can be hiked or biked for about 12 km before it turns somewhat vague although it can be continued much further if desired.

A large muddy area is found almost immediately after starting down the road. Pick your way through and fear not, as this is about as bad as it gets. A number of other swampy areas will have to be passed through further down, particularly around the low pass about 4 km in. The mighty spires of Mount Monolith can be seen several km down the road. Several more km in, the impressive north face of Mount Robert Henderson (see previous page) comes into view, and at about the 10 km point, views of the magnificent jagged subpeaks of Trapper Mountain can be seen to the north. This is a good turn-around point as the road then drops in elevation and becomes quite washed out. Return by same route.

A herd of woodland (aka mountain) caribou, the 1200 member Hart River herd, can sometimes be seen in this area. The herd is experiencing some pressure from over- hunting, a pattern found in a number of areas in the Yukon. Another large herd of caribou, the Porcupine herd, numbers around 160,000 and is composed of the Woodland caribou's smaller cousin, the barrenground caribou.

The entire Porcupine herd crosses the Dempster Highway every fall and is a stunning sight. Named after the Porcupine River near Old Crow, this herd is also feeling pressures, this time from proposed oil development in their calving range. The Gwich' inn of Old Crow would be hit the hardest as this mighty herd has sustained them for thousands of years.

Hike 3: Angelcomb Mountain. Medium/ Hard. 6 km, 3-4 hours return, and an elevation gain of 2200 feet.

NOTE: Please avoid this hike in spring-to-early summer when the sheep are lambing. If you do see sheep later in the season, please give them ample room.

From the Tombstone campground (71.5 km up the Dempster Highway), drive for just over 10 km to a large gravel pit on your right. Ignore a smaller pullover about ½ km before it. The parking loop is found just before the road drops steeply into the valley below. Look for a sign showing a pair of binoculars, which are a good recommendation.

Check for two inviting ridges that descend close to the highway; the one on the left is steeper than the one on the right. The right ridge is the one you're after. Several braided horse trails that lead up this ridge are located in the far (southeast) corner of the parking area.

The horse trails soon converge into one trail which leads up the obvious ridge system to the viewpoint. Approximately ½ hour up, a rocky look-out is reached. This is a possible turn-around.

The trail passes some surreal looking rock hoodoos as it continues upward. As the summit is approached, the trail becomes quite indistinct; try to stay high on the ridge. The steepest section is found just before reaching the subpeak. Return by the same route.

The unusual rocky outcrops found on this hike are known as castellations and are a type of hoodoo. They are formed when softer rock is eroded away from harder material. Fantastic examples can be found throughout the southern and northern Ogilvies ranges.

More Options: The whole area to the north of North Fork Pass has excellent hiking potential. Peaks and ridges in this area look very approachable. This is true to a degree. The tundra can sometimes be excellent to walk on, but can also hold a lot of moisture, can have very uneven ground, and be a mecca for mosquitos. Once the base of a mountain is reached the hiking becomes much better. There are often many choices for routes along the various ridge systems. Please tread lightly on the tundra whenever possible.

Ed Vos

Hoodoos, a type of castellation, and other exposed rock formations give the Ogilvie Range a distinctive air.

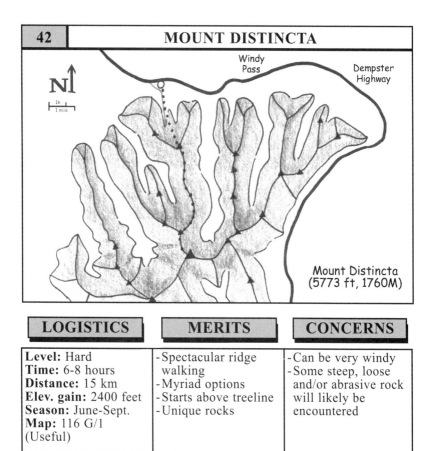

LOGISTICS	MERITS	CONCERNS

Level: Hard
 Time: 6-8 hours
 Distance: 15 km
 Elev. gain: 2400 feet
 Season: June-Sept.
 Map: 116 G/1
 (Useful)
	- Spectacular ridge
	   walking
	 - Myriad options
	 - Starts above treeline
	 - Unique rocks
		- Can be very windy
		 - Some steep, loose
		   and/or abrasive rock
		   will likely be
		   encountered

Drive up the Dempster Highway past the Tombstone Campground (km 71.5) to km 155, about 3 km past Windy Pass. An 'Ogilvie' maintenance gravel pit on your left signals the approach of a small hard to spot parking area less than a km down, which is also on your left.

Look for a creek that heads in a southernly direction from the parking area. The walking is good for several kilometres as elevation is slowly gained. Keep your eyes open for a gently rising rocky ridge to your left. Leave the creek and follow this ridge to a steep talus climb due south. This is easily the hardest part of the hike and can take some time to ascend.

Upon reaching the top of the climb, the peak of Mount Distincta comes into view, as well as a number of very inviting ridge systems. Continue towards the summit by following the obvious ridge to your left. Walking is efficient and wonderful for several km as Distincta's peak draws closer. It is another rocky climb to the summit, but shorter than the first big elevation gain, and this is rewarded by stunning panoramic views of the north and south Ogilvie Mountains. Return by the same route or check out the following Option.

Option: Distincta Ridge Systems. Hard. Time and distance are variable, use your own discretion.

By taking a look at the map one can chose numerous ridge-walking options. "Octopus Mountain" is a more appropriate name for this massif due to the many rocky arms that spread out in all directions from the peak. Be aware of some tricky scree/talus sections when choosing a route, as well as the distance back to your vehicle and the highway.

View Explained: The summit of Mount Distincta allows for sweeping views of the North and South Ogilvie Ranges. Looking to the east towards the mountains across the highway, colourful bands of rock can be seen. Pilot Mountain, also known as Vine Mountain, can be spotted further down the highway, to the southeast. Numerous hoodoos (rock towers) found on this summit give the mountain a unique appearance. Pilots often use this distinct landmark for navigational purposes, hence the name.

Due south lie the verdant meadows of the Blackstone Plateau. This is an excellent habitat for the area's population of moose. Further south lie the jagged peaks of the Southern Ogilvies and to the north the grey ridge systems of the Northern Ogilvies.

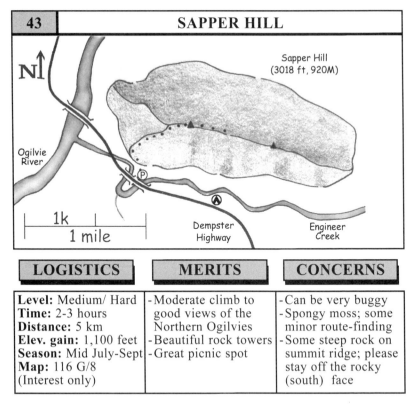

LOGISTICS	**MERITS**	**CONCERNS**
Level: Medium/ Hard **Time:** 2-3 hours **Distance:** 5 km **Elev. gain:** 1,100 feet **Season:** Mid July-Sept **Map:** 116 G/8 (Interest only)	- Moderate climb to good views of the Northern Ogilvies - Beautiful rock towers - Great picnic spot	- Can be very buggy - Spongy moss; some minor route-finding - Some steep rock on summit ridge; please stay off the rocky (south) face

NOTE: A Peregrine Falcon raises her young on the southeast face of Sapper Hill. Peregrines are VERY susceptible to disturbances and must be given ample room. These falcons have been known to dislodge their eggs if encroached upon. Avoid this hike until mid-July and DO NOT venture any further than the route indicated on the map (there is (was?) a sign posted there). Since this nest is of historical significance (it was producing young when peregrine populations hit a frightening low) there is a good chance this route will be closed to hiking if this habitat is not respected.

Drive to the Engineer Creek campground which is located at km 194 on the Dempster Highway. From here drive, walk or bike a little under one km north to a parking area on your right just past a small bridge. A very vague trail can be picked up due east (at a right angle to the highway). Hike through the forest in a southeast direction until a craggy rock tower comes into view. Head up towards it through the mossy forest. Upon reaching this landmark, the way becomes obvious. Numerous viewpoints and rest spots can be found along the ridge. Some scrambling further along may intimidate some and delight others. The ridge can be followed for almost 1 km before it begins to drop downwards. Any point along the ridge can serve as a convenient turn-around point. Although it's possible to drop down onto the west face of Sapper Hill and then back to the campground, this option entails some nasty terrain and a formidable creek crossing. There is also a falcon nest on the west face that should be given ample room.

Option: Mount Jekyll. Very Hard. 14 km and 7-9 hours return.

This challenging hike, which is not shown on the map, offers excellent views and options. There are some amazing hoodoos found along the ridge as well as other incredible rock formations. I highly recommend acquiring the topographical map listed on the previous page.

From the Engineer Creek campground drive or bike 4 km north. Look for a pull-over near where the road widens. Hike into the swampy forest in a westward direction. Continue northwest until you reach a mossy saddle and Mount Jekyll's south arm comes into view. Follow it up as long as you desire. The summit, marked by a large rock cairn, is a long day-hike away.

Peregrine falcons can sometimes be spotted gliding over Sapper Hill as well as over much of the Dempster Highway and surrounding areas. Often acknowledged as the fastest creature on the planet, it is capable of reaching speeds of up to 300 km per hour! The falcon hunts ground squirrels, ptarmigan, ducks, and a number of smaller birds.

This amazing and beautiful bird has experienced pressure in its southern range, but populations are more stable in the north and closely follow the cycles of the ptarmigan, their exclusive winter food. This hardy bird is a true 'sourdough', sticking out the long, cold and dark northern winter.

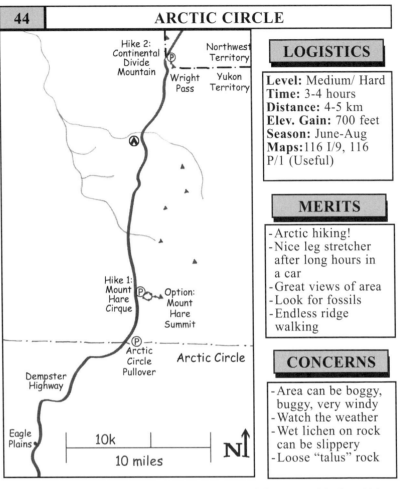

Hike 2:
Continental
Divide
Mountain

Northwest
Territory

Wright
Pass

Yukon
Territory

Hike 1:
Mount
Hare
Cirque

Option:
Mount
Hare
Summit

Arctic
Circle
Pullover

Arctic Circle

Dempster
Highway

Eagle
Plains

10k

10 miles

N

LOGISTICS

Level: Medium/ Hard
Time: 3-4 hours
Distance: 4-5 km
Elev. Gain: 700 feet
Season: June-Aug
Maps:116 I/9, 116
P/1 (Useful)

MERITS

- Arctic hiking!
- Nice leg stretcher
  after long hours in
  a car
- Great views of area
- Look for fossils
- Endless ridge
  walking

CONCERNS

- Area can be boggy,
  buggy, very windy
- Watch the weather
- Wet lichen on rock
  can be slippery
- Loose "talus" rock

NOTE: Easily accessible ridges can be found from roughly km 410 to km 426.

Hike 1: Mount Hare Cirque. Medium/ Hard. 5 km and 3 hours return.

The trailhead is found 7 km from the Arctic Circle, which is obviously a must stop photo shoot, on the right. Drive down the road to the end of the gravel pit.

Two ridge systems present themselves to you from here. The closest one on the left is a good place to start the circuit. Follow the ridge to the first descent, a fair decline in elevation. Continue along the ridge while occasionally sidehilling around the sub-peaks. An obvious ridge system leading to the true summit of Mount Hare connects from the east. Consider the Option which starts here or continue around the cirque.

Once again some drops and gains in elevation will be encountered. Pick your line down to the creek and back to the parking area.

Option: Mount Hare Summit. Medium/ Hard. Add 5 km and up to 4 hours to Hike 1.

The route from here is straightforward with strong winds and steep loose rock being the main obstacles. The views are excellent with much potential for further exploration.

Hike 2: Continental Divide Summit. Medium/Hard. 4 km and 2- 3 hours return.

Wright Pass, which separates the Yukon from the Northwest Territories, can be found at km 465 on the Dempster Highway. Ample parking is found in either Territory. (I advise avoiding the hiking route directly north from the pass, due to unstable rocks).

Look for a line of ascent up the ridge to the south, opposite the road and station. Unfortunately the terrain (grassy sections and rock) is a little trickier to traverse than it first appears. Nonetheless, the approach is short and the climb up large loose pieces of talus begins. Follow either the ridge line or a grassy section to the right of it. An occasional rock cairn can be seen until the summit is reached which is marked by more cairns and a great 360 degree view.

The Arctic Circle, a must stop for all initiates.

CHAPTER 6

TRAVEL INFORMATION

Courtesy of Yukon Archives

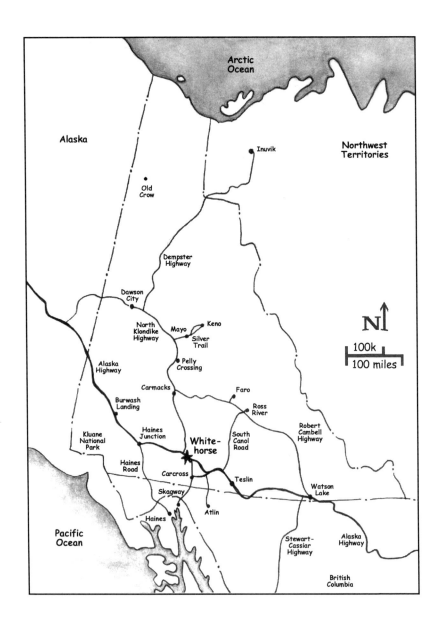

YUKON AND AREA HIGHWAYS & ROADS

Name	Length	Speed limit	Open	Surface	Ferries
Alaska Highway	1057 km	90-100 km	Year-round	Mainly asphalt	None
Klondike Highway	717 km	90 km	Year-round	Mainly asphalt	One
Haines Road	256 km	90-100 km	Year-round	Asphalt	None
Cambell Highway	582 km	90 km	Year-round	Asphalt	None
Haines Road	256 km	90-100 km	Year-round	Mainly gravel	None
Dempster Highway	741 km	70-90 km	Year-round	Mainly gravel	Two
South Canol Rd.	224 km	60 km	Summer	Gravel	None
Atlin Road	90 km	80 km	Year-round	Ashphalt and gravel	None
Silver Trail	112 km	Up to 90 km	Year-round	Asphalt and gravel	None
Top of the World	66 km	40-60 km	Summer	Gravel	One

* Yukon portion

DRIVING TIPS

•Drive with headlights on at all times. This increases your and others' visibility.

•Watch for loose gravel, dust, muddy sections and nasty weather.

•Also watch for bikers, road crews and large mammals.

•Gas stations, hospitals and help can be hours away; be prepared.

•Be realistic about distances. Pull over if fatigued.

•Travel with spares and extra gas, oil and windshield wiper fluid.

•Phone Highways Yukon (668-6061) for current road conditions.

•Cold weather drivers should be prepared to survive a breakdown; take matches, candles, sleeping bags, axe, radio etc.

COMMUNITIES

All communities have banks and post offices, many with irregular hours.

Town	Population	Police/ Emergency	Radio	Visitor Centre
Atlin	450	651-7511 651-7700	90.1 FM	651-7522
Carcross	450	821-5555 821-4444	96.1FM	821-4431
Carmacks	500	863-5555 863-4444	990 AM	863-6606
Dawson City	2,150	993-5555 993-4444	560AM 98.7FM	993-5566
Faro	350	994-5555 994-4444	105.1 FM	994-2728
Haines, Alaska	2,300	911	700 AM	766-2234
Haines Junction	850	634-5555 634-4444	103.5 FM	634-2345
Inuvik, N.W.T.	3200	979-2935 979-2955		979-4518
Mayo	500	996-5555 996-4444	1230 AM	996-2317
Ross River	450	996-5555 996-4444	98.7 FM	
Skagway, Alaska	750	911	98.7 FM	983-2854
Teslin	450	390-5555 390-4444	940 AM	
Watson Lake	1,800	390-5555 390-4444	990 AM	536-7469
White-Horse	24,000	911	570 AM, 98.7 FM, 98.1 FM	667-2915

Keno City, Old Crow, Burwash Landing, Pelly Crossing, Tagish, Beaver Creek, Stewart Crossing and Destruction Bay are not listed above.

Town	Hostel	Showers Laundry	Public Pool	Museum Library	Equipmemt Rentals
Atlin	No	Showers, Laundry	No	Museum, Library	Bikes, Canoes, Kayaks
Carcross	No	Showers, Laundry	Otdoor	651-7522	Arrange rentals in Whitehorse
Carmacks	No	Showers, Laundry	Outdoor	Library	Arrange rentals in Whitehorse
Dawson City	Yes	Showers, Laundry	Outdoor	Museum, Library	Bikes, Canoes
Faro	No	Showers, Laundry	No	Interpretive Centre	
Haines, Alaska	Yes	Showers, Laundry		Museum	Bikes, Canoes, Kayaks
Haines Junction	No	Showers, Laundry		Library	Canoes
Inuvik, N.W.T.	No	Showers, Laundry		Library	Canoes, Kayaks
Mayo	No	Showers, Laundry	Outdoor	Library	
Ross River	No	Laundry		Library	
Skagway, Alaska	Yes	Showers, Laundry		Museum, Library	Bikes
Teslin	No	Showers, Laundry		Museum, Library	Bikes, Canoes
Watson Lake	No	Showers, Laundry	Indoor	Museum, Library	Bikes, Canoes
White- horse	Yes	Showers, Laundry	Indoor	Museums, Library	Bikes, Canoes, Kayaks

Town	Attractions	Festivals, Events
Atlin, BC	Historic buildings, fishing & boating, dinner theatre	Canada Day, Atlin Day celebrations- July 1st
Carcross	Native dancing, Mounties' barracks, "mini-desert"	
Carmacks	Rock displays in Visitor centre, lots of short trails	
Dawson City	Historic buildings, tours, gambling, poetry recitals	Music Festival 3rd week of July; Outhouse races
Faro	Wildlife viewing stations	Faro/ Ross River summer Arts Festival- early June
Haines Junction	Kluane Park Centre, films, and walking tours, bakery	"Alsek" Music Festival mid-June; Mountain Festival
Inuvik, NWT	The "Igloo" church and other interesting buildings	Great Northern Arts Festival- late July
Mayo	Good museum, lots of old roads for biking in area	Mayo Mountain Maniac Triathlon- early/mid August
Ross River	Suspension bridge, historic native village	Ross River Dena Cultural Exchange: mid to late July
Skagway, Alaska	Historic buildings, museums, theatre, boat tours	Independance Day parade Jul 4, Garden/Craft Fair: mid-August
Teslin	Excellent Museum, Fishing, Native Crafts	Canada Day fishing derby, Winter carnival (March)
Watson Lake	Northern Lights Centre, 'sign post forest'	Open golf tournament- May. Canada Day celebrations
White-horse	Art galleries, theatres, 3 museums, free guided hikes, Goldrush entertainment, Berengia Center	Frostbite Music Festival: mid-February. Storytelling Festival: mid-June. Winter Carnival (Rendezvous): February

CAMPGROUNDS

Yukon government-run campgrounds are in bold print. They offer wood, shelters (at most locations), fire pits, picnic tables and outhouses. Seasonal passes are available.

The RV campgrounds mentioned below have tent camping as well.

NOTE: Mileposts (Km) may vary due to recent road construction. All campgrounds are marked. Price and quality of campsites vary.

ALASKA HIGHWAY

Campground	Km	Campground	Km
Watson Lake	1025+a	**Aishihik Lake**	1590+e
Greenvalley RV Park	1032	**Pine Lake**	1628
Upper Liard	1033	Kluane RV	1636
Rancheria Motel	1144	Macintosh Lodge	1646
Morley River Lodge	1252	Bayshore Lodge	1712
Dawson Peak Lodge	1282	Cottonwood Park	1717
Teslin Lake	1309	**Congdon Creek**	1723
Squanga Lake	1368	Selja Services Park	1743
Lakeview Resort	1413	Kluane Dalan Park	1759
Marsh Lake	1430	Pine Valley Motel	1844
Sourdough	1453	**Lake Creek**	1854
Wolfe Creek	1459	Koidern River Lodge	1872
Robert Service	1470+b	**Snag Junction**	1913
Takhini River	1543+c	Ida's Motel	1934
Kusawa Lake	1543+d		

a) + 1.5 km on acess road
b) + 2 km on South Access (Robert Service Way) Road
c) + 15 km on Kusawa Lake Road
d) + 23 km on Kusawa Lake Road
e) + 42 km on Aishihik Lake Road

Campground	Km	Campground	Km

ATLIN ROAD

Campground	Km	Campground	Km
Snafu	26	Surprise Lake	92+a
Tarfu	33	Grotto	92+b

a) + 1 km on Warm Bay Road
b) + 19 km on Warm Bay Road

ROBERT CAMBELL HIGHWAY

Campground	Km	Campground	Km
Simpson Lake	81	John Connoly Park	427+b
Frances Lake	175	**Drury Lake**	483
Lapie Canyon	364	**Little Salmon Lake**	517
Johnson Lake	427+a		

a) + 4 km on Faro Road
b) + 10 km on Faro Road

HAINES ROAD

Campground	Km	Campground	Km
Kathleen Lake	27	Salmon Run RV	245
Dezadeash Lake	51	Portage Cove	244
Million Dollar Falls	89	Bear Creek Hostel	244+a
Mosquito Lake	200		

a) + 2 km on Mud Bay Road & Small Tracts Road

SOUTH CANOL ROAD

Campground	Km	Campground	Km
Johnsons Crossing	0	**Quiet Lake**	77

SILVER TRAIL ROAD

Campground	Km	Campground	Km
5 Mile Lake	57	Keno City	112

Campground	Km	Campground	Km

SOUTH KLONDIKE HIGHWAY

Campground	Km	Campground	Km
Hanousek Park	0	Liarville	4
Dyea National Park	3.5+a	**Carcross**	106

a) +13 km on Dyea Road

NORTH KLONDIKE HIGHWAY

Campground	Km	Campground	Km
Takhini Hot Springs	6+a	**Ethel Lake**	333+c
Lake Laberge	33+b	Wispering Willows	344
Fox Lake	56	**Moose Creek**	369
Twin Lakes	116	McQuesten	391
Carmacks	165	**Dempster Corner**	485
Tatchun Creek	191	**Klondike River**	507
Minto Landing	238	Guggieville RV	522
Pelly Crossing	272	Yukon River	525+d

a) + 10 km on the Takini Hot Springs Road.
b) + 3 km on Deep Creek Road
c) + 24 km on Ethel Lake Road
d)This campground is located across the Yukon River from Dawson

DEMPSTER HIGHWAY

Campground	Km	Campground	Km
Tombstone	71	Nitanlaii	540
Engineer Creek	194	Caribou Creek	686
Eagle Plains	369	Chuk	730
Rock River	447	Inuvik	735

PARKS AND PROTECTED AREAS

Kluane National Park was established in 1972 and is co-managed by Parks Canada, the Champagne/Aishihik and Kluane First Nations. Canada's highest peaks and part of the world's largest non-polar icefields and are found in the park boundaries.

Kluane is home to abundant wildlife, with the highest concentration of Dall Sheep and Grizzly Bears in the Yukon.

Registration and the use of bear canisters is mandatory for overnight trips. Parks Canada operates a visitor and registration centre in Haines Junction; it is open year-round. Department of Canadian Heritage, Yukon District, Parks Canada, 205-300 Main Street, Whitehorse, Yukon, Y1A 2B5 ~ 667-3910 Kluane National Park and Reserve, PO Box 5495, Haines Junction, YOB 1LO ~ 634-7209

Chilkoot National Historic Park is jointly maintained by Parks Canada and United States National Park Services for its exceptional cultural, historical and recreational value. Opened as a park in the 1960's the Chilkoot Pass has become a major northern attraction.
Department of Canadian Heritage (above).

Tatshenshini Provincial Park was established in 1996 to protect the unique and wild Alsek and Tatshenshini River system from development. The Park is popular for whitewater rafting and for lengthy wilderness tours. Guides are available in Whitehorse and Haines Junction.
The Park is jointly managed by the Champagne/Aishihik Band and BC Parks. The park connects with Kluane National Park and neighboring Wrangell/ Saint Elias Park in Alaska. All three comprise the largest protected area in the world!
BC Parks ~ Skeena District. Bag 5000, Smithers, B.C. V0J 2N0

Atlin Provincial Park protects part of Atlin Lake, British Columbia's largest freshwater lake, and the Lewellen Glacier, part of the enormous Juneau ice cap. There are no trails and no park staff. Lake kayaking and heli-hiking are popular ways of seeing this remote wilderness park. Contact: Same as Tatshenshini Park (above).

Tombstone Territorial Park is an over 2000 square kilometer wilderness area recently protected from development. Contact box 2703, Whitehorse, YT, Y1A 2C6. Phone: 667-5639.

NOTE: There are numerous other protected areas in the Yukon. Contact Parks Canada or Renewable Resources for more information.

CONSERVATION

Renewable Resources provides a number of wilderness-related services, such as wildlife viewing programs, the issuing of hunting and fishing licences, and wildlife and habitat recovery programs. RR also produces some excellent free brochures (like the *Yukon Wildlife Viewing Guide*, and *Into the Yukon Wilderness*), as welll as making and maintaining some of the excellent walking trails found in this guide. Departments of RR are found in numerous Yukon communities. They are helpful for general inquiries. 10 Burns Road, Whitehorse (across from the airport)
667- 5652. Explore the Wild (free tours and talks) 1-800-661-0408 toll free.

Yukon Conservation Society: "YCS" as it is known locally, has been involved with conservation issues since 1968. YCS offers a number of free guided tours in the Whitehorse area (e.g. Canyon City, Clay Cliffs, Long Lake, Yukon River, Hidden Lakes, Haekel Hill) throughout the summer. Volunteers are always welcomed and the Society operates out of an office which doubles as a drop-in resource centre.
302 Hawkins Street, Whitehorse, YT. Box 4163, Y1A 3S9. (867) 668-5678 E-mail: ycs@polarcom.com

Canadian Parks and Wilderness Society: The Yukon Chapter of CPAWS is actively involved in a number of conservation programs like the Yukon Protected Areas Strategy, the Y2Y (Yukon to Yellowknife) initiative, and the Wildlands Project. CPAWS also works towards establishing protected areas and viable wildlife corridors.
P.O. Box 31095, 209 Lowe Street, Whitehorse, Yukon Y1A 5P7 (867) 393-8080 E-mail: cpaws@yknet.ca

Friends of Yukon Rivers work for river and watershed protection. Together with YCS and CPAWS (see above) they form the Yukon Wildlands Project. "FOYR" are also involved in numerous concert fund-raisers. 668-7370

Fish and Game Association: Since 1945 the YFGA has focused on outdoor wilderness recreation and educational programs. 667-4263

Raven Recycling offers a wide range of waste diversion programs as well as general recycling. 100 Galena Road, Whitehorse. 667-7269

TRAVEL INFORMATION

Flights: Canadian Airlines~ 1-800-665-1177 (year-round)
Canada 3000 ~ 1-888-241-1997 (book through agent; summer only)
Condor Air (European Direct) ~ 1-800-524-6975 (summer only)

Small Aircraft: In addition to Air North a number of bush pilots can be hired for heli-hiking, canoe drop offs and pick ups.
Air North ~ 668-2228 www.airnorth.yk.net 1-800-661-0407 in Canada.

Ferries: Alaska and British Columbia Ferries connect the Yukon to the Pacific Seaboard.
Alaska Marine Highway ~ 1-800-642-0066 in Canada and the U.S.
B.C. Ferries 1-888-223-3779, British Columbia. 1-250-386-3431 outside BC.

Trains: One tourist train connects Skagway to British Columbia. The train can also be used by Chilkoot hikers to get back to Alaska; the trip is beautiful but pricey. White Pass and Yukon Route 1-800-343-7373

Bus lines: Bus lines connect the Yukon communities to Alaska and British Columbia. Greyhound 1-800-661-1145.

Vehicle Rentals: Whitehorse has a good selection of vehicle rentals. There may be difficulties encountered with taking rentals across borders.

Carpooling: Carpooling on hiking trips and for general travel saves gas, money and is easier on the environment. Billboards at Visitor Centres and local cafes can be good places for those looking to set up a ride or to take riders. This is usually preferable to hitchhiking.

Banking: International travelers should be aware that it may be difficult to exchange currency in many banks. U.S. or Canadian Travel cheques are best. All communities listed on page 166 have banks.
NOTE: Smaller towns have very irregular banking hours.

Medical Care: Only Whitehorse is equipped to deal with serious emergencies. If traveling from outside Canada, it is highly recommended that you have proper medical insurance obtained beforehand. See page 166 for Hospitals and Nursing Centres.
NOTE: All numbers are Whitehorse area unless otherwise noted.

CONTACT NUMBERS

Emergency/ Travel Conditions
Police/ Medical ~ See Communities page 166.
Forest Fires ~ 668-2263 or dial O; ask for Zenith 5555
Whitehorse Area Weather ~ 668-8424
Road Conditions ~ 456-7623
Dempster Highway Road and Ferry Report ~ 1 (800) 661-0752
Borders (US-Canada) ~ 821-4111

History/ Culture
Yukon Historical and Museums Association ~ 667-4704
Yukon Archives ~ 667-5321
Yukon Native Language Centre ~ 668-8820
First Nations Tourism ~ 667-7698

Guided Tours, Tour Guides
Free Guided Tours ~ Contact YCS or Renewable Resources (page 173).
Wilderness Tourism Association of the Yukon ~ 1-800-221-3880.

Maps & Books - Ordering
Macs Fireweed ~ 668-6104; North America Toll Free ~ 1-800-661-0508
Maximilian's Goldrush Emporium (Dawson, books, maps) ~ 993-5486
Madley's General Store ~ (Haines Junction, some books, maps) 634-2200.
Geological Survey of Canada Bookstore (maps): 101-605 Robson Street, Vancouver, BC V6B 5J3.

Outfitting - Gear
Coast Mountain Sports ~ 667-4074
Valhalla Pure ~ 668-7700
Sportslodge Source for Sports ~ 668-6848
Second Time Around Sports ~ 668-3565
Trading Post (Dawson) ~ 993-5316
Canadian Tire ~ 668-3652

Clubs, Sports and Leisure
Sports Yukon (General) ~ 668-4236

NOTE: Sports Yukon has current contact numbers of the many clubs (running, bike-racing, hiking, climbing, canoeing/ kayaking, orienteering, birding, skiing, biathlon, dog-mushing etc.) in the Territory.

RECOMMENDED READING

Ordering: Macs Fireweed in downtown Whitehorse carries most of the books listed here, as well as topographical maps. Books and maps can be ordered via the Internet or through the mail. See previous page for addresses.

Yukon, History

-**The Lost Moose Catalogue(s)** by assorted authors; Lost Moose Publishing.
-**The Yukon Fact Book** by Mark Zuehlke; Whitecap Books.
-**The Colorful Five Percent(s)** by Jim Robb; Colorful Five Percent Co.
-**Part of the Land, Part of the Water** (First Nations) by Catherine McCellan; Douglas and MacIntyre.
-**Life Lived Like a Story** (First Nations) by Julie Cruikshank; UBS Press.
-**Klondike Ho!** by Curtis Vos; Lost Moose Publishing.
-**Klondike** by Pierre Berton; McClelland & Stewart.
-**Chilkoot Trail** by David Neufield/ Frank Norris; Lost Moose Publishing.
-**Klondike Women** by Melanie J. Mayer; Ohio University Press.

Naturalism

-**Flora of the Yukon** by T. William, J. Cody; National Research Canada
-**Wildflowers of the Yukon, Alaska and Northwestern Canada** by John Trelawny; Sono Nis Press.
-**Plants of the Western Boreal Forest & Aspen Parkland** by Assorted Authors; Lone Pine.
-**Edible and Medicinal Plants** by Terry Willard Ph.D.; Wild Rose Books
-**All the Rain Promises and more...** (Mushrooms) by David Aurora; Ten Speed Press/ Biosystems Books.
-**Field Guide to Western Birds** by Audubon; McGraw Hill National.
-**Birds of the Dempster** by Robert Firsh; Morris Print Company.
-**Birds of Swan Lake** by Helmut Grunberg/ Key Line Graphic Design.
-**Field Guide to North American Mammals** by Alfred A. Knopf; Audubon Society Chanticleer Press.
-**Tracking and the Art of Seeing** by Paul Rezendes; Harper Perennial.
-**Rocks and Minerals** by Discovery Books.
-**The Aurora Watchers Handbook** by Neil Davis; University of Alaska Press.
- **Exploring the Night Sky** by Terence Dickinson; Camden House.

Hiking

-**Whitehorse and Area Hikes and Bikes** by the Yukon Conservation Society; Lost Moose Publishing.
-**Kluane National Park Hiking Guide** by Vivian Lougheed; New Star Books.
-**Along the Dempster** by Walter Lanz; Oak House Publishing.
-**Whitehorse Trail Map** by the Government of Yukon, City of Whitehorse, Renewable Resources, Parks and Recreation.
-**Leave No Trace** by Annette McGivny; Backpacker & Mountaineers.
-**Everyday Wisdom (1001 expert tips for hikers)** by Karen Berger; Backpacker/ Mountaineers.
-**Be Expert with Map and Compass** by Bjorn Kjellstrom.
-**GPS Made Easy** by Laurence Letham; Rocky Mountain Books.
-**Backcountry Bear Basics** by Dave Smith; Greystone Publishers.
-**Saint Johns Ambulance Official Wilderness First Aid Guide** by Wayne Merry; McClelland and Stewart Inc.

Other Outdoor Sports

-**The Yukon River** by Mike Rourke; Rivers of the North Publications.
-**The Teslin River** by Gus Carpes; Kugh Enterprises.
-**The Big Salmon River,** and **The Nisutlin River** by Gus Carpes; Kugh Enterprises.
-**Rivers of the Yukon** by Ken Madsen; Primrose Press.
-**Tatshenshini Wilderness Quest** by Ken Madsen; Primrose Press.
-**The Wind, the Snake and the Bonnet Plume** by Friends of Yukon Rivers & CPAWS Yukon.
-**Nahanni, River of Dreams** by Neil Hartling; The Canadian Recreational Canoeing Association.
-**Hot Springs of Western Canada** by Glenn Woodsworth; Gordon Soules.
-**Guide to Single Pitch Climbs of the Yukon** by Greg Keitel and Alan Pohl; Rock'n Rave'n
-**The Rock Gardens** by Alain Delaire; Outdoor Pursuits/ F.H. Collins.
-**Skijor with your Dog** by Hoe-Raitto/ Kayno; OK Publishing

In addition to these books consider ordering these **FREE** publications:
- **Guide to the Goldfields**; Harper Street Publishing. 1-867-993-6671; e:mail: goldfields@dawson.net
- **Yukon Vacation Guide** by Tourism Yukon. 1-867-667-534 ~ e:mail ~hsp@alaskayukon.com

GLOSSARY

Alpine: Environment found above the treeline on mountains.
Arctic Circle: Imaginary line at 66.33 degrees latitude.
Aurora Borealis: Northern lights; see page 17.
Avalanche: A volume of tumbling snow and/or rock.
Bearing: Sense of direction, reading from compass.
Beaver fever: See Giardia.
Boreal: Northern.
Boot-skiing: Skiing down snow or rock on boots.
Burn: Former forest recently razed by fire.
Buckbrush: Large shrubs like willow, alder and dwarf birch.
Bushwhack: Off-trail travel usually through vegetation.
Cache: A stash-place for food and/or gear; often on stilts.
Cairn: Pile of rocks used for navigation or for marking a summit.
Cirque: Bowl-like depression high in the mountains.
Castellations: Rocky towers, hoodoos.
Compass: Navigational device with arrow that points north; very handy
Contour line: Map lines that measure elevation differences.
Declination (magnetic): True north as opposed to map north.
Drainage: Usually refers to a creek drainage, ravine, or gully.
Exposure: Refers to either hypothermia or steep relief.
Giardia: Nasty parasite found in some bodies of water.
G.P.S. Global Positioning System; digital unit uses satellite technology.
High country: Subalpine or alpine environment.
Hypothermia: Cooling of body core; See page 43.
Igneous: Volcanic rock.
Magnetic North: See page 36.
Map North: "True North; see page 36.
Metamorphic: Rock formed by heat and/or pressure.
Permafrost: Permanently frozen ground.
Raptors: Carnivorous hunting and scavenging birds.
Single-Track: Footpaths preferred by seasoned mountain bikers.
Sedimentary: Rock formed by deposition of organic materials.
Scree: Loose alpine rock, smaller than fist size.
Side-hilling: Traveling sideways across a hill or mountain.
Taiga: Northern boreal forest.
Talus: Loose alpine rock, larger than fist size.
Topography: Variables in terrain.
Tree-line: Imaginary line where the forest ends.
True North: Magnetic North. See page 36.
Tundra: Vegetated treeless zone common above the Arctic Circle.
Tussocks: Unstable protruding mats of grass and sedges.Alaska

FIRST NATIONS PLACE NAMES

Aishihik - (S. Tutchone) - Name of the village.

Alsek - (Tlingit) - Resting place.

Atlin - (Tlingit) - Big lake

Dezedeash - (Tlingit) - Shortage of snares.

Dene - (Kaska and Tagish) - The people.

Donjek - (N. Tutchone) - Indian berry.

Klondike - (Han) - Stone hammer.

Kluane - (S. Tutchone) - Home of small white fish.

Kusawa - (Tlingit) - Narrow lake.

Nahanni - (Dene) - Regional name for strangers, enemy tribes.

Takhini - (Tlingit) - Hot (spings) water.

Yukon - (Han) - White water river, the great river.

Mussi cho (a big thank you) to the Aboriginal Language Services.

INDEX

Alsek Road 110-111
Agate/ Gem Trails 132-133
Amphitheatre Mountain .122,126
Athapaskan (language) . . .25-27
Atlin 52, 58, 178-180
Atlin Lake 58, 59
Atlin Road 52, 58
Arctic Circle 128, 160
Arctic Grayling 20
Aurora Borealis 17
Auriol Trail 108

Backcountry Skiing 48
Badlands Creek 122-126
Battery Point 92
Bear Creek 112
Bears 22, 35, 39-41,
Beringia 22
Bering land bridge 25
Biking 45
Birds 21
Blueberry Hill 150
Black Bears . . . .(see bears)
Bonanza Road 140-141
Bonneville Lakes 70-71
Buckbrush 11, 42
Bullion Creek 114, 118
Burwash Creek 122-126
Burwash Loop 90
Burwash Glacier 126
Burwash Uplands 122-124

Canyon City 62-63
Cantlie Lake 64-65
Campfires 18-38
Carcross (town) .76-79, 166-168
Carcross walks 76-79
Caribou 22-23, 154
Caribou Mountain 77
Carmacks 128-129, 133
Campgrounds 169-171
Canada Creek 114-116

Clay Cliffs 60
Climbing (rock) 47
Clouds 17, 33
Chadburn Lake 67-67
Chadden Lake 66-67
Chilkat Pass 96-97
Chilkoot Pass 84-88, 184
Coal Lake 70-73
Coal Lake Road 70, 73
Compass 36, 140
Congdon Creek 120-121
Continental Divide Summit .160
Cottonwood Trail 102-105
CPAWS 173
Creek Crossings 42
Crocus Bluffs 47, 142,-143
Cross Country Skiing 48, 49

Dawson City 128, 142
Dempster Highway 129, 146-161
Dewey Lakes (Upper, Lower) .82
Devils Punchbowl 82
Dezadeash Lake 100
Dezadeash River 110-11
Dike Hike 142-143
Discovery Ridge 150-151
Divide Lake 148-149
Dog Mushing 48-49
Donjek Glacier 122-126
Duke River 122-123
Dyea Road 84-86

Fannin Sheep Trails 134-135
Faro 134-135
Feather Peak 80-81
Fireweed 18, 19
First Aid 43, 177
First Nations . . .9, 14, 19, 24-27
Fish Lake 52, 70-73
Fish/Fishing 20, 29
Five Finger Rapids 130-131

Gear 30,34,35
Glissade Pass 146-149
Gold 15
Golden Horn Mountain . . .70-73
Goldensides Mountain . .152-153
Grey Mountain 64, 65
Grizzly bears *(see bears)*
Grizzly Lake 149-149
Gwich' inn 24-27, 154

Han 24-27
Haines Junction 90,91
Haines Pass *(see Chilkat Pass)*
Haines Road 90, 91
Haines, Alaska 90, 91
Hart River Road 152-154
Heli-pad Viewpoint 96-97
Hidden Lakes 667, 67
Hoge Pass 122, 125
Hunting 39
Hypothermia 43, 48

Ibex area Mountain 68, 69
Ibex Valley 52, 68, 69
Icy Lake 82-83
Inland Tlingit 24-27

Jakes Corner 56
Jones Gap 94, 95

Lake Bennett 85, 88
Liard River 16, 54, 55
Log Cabin 49
Long Lake 44, 60, 61
Lucky Lake 54, 44

Kathleen Lake 104, 106
Kaska 24, 27
Kaskawulsh Glacier 16
Keno 128, 139-139
Kimberly Meadows 113
King Solomon's Dome 141

Kings Throne 106, 107
Klondike goldrush .14, 28, 63, 75
Klondike Campground Loop .142
Kluane National Park .14, 15, 30
Kusawa Lake 16, 90

Mackenzie River 16
Magnussen Trail 64, 65
Maps 10, 11, 36
Mayo 2, 128, 136, 178-180
Midnight Sun 17
Midnight Dome 14, 17
Miles Canyon 52, 62, 63
Million Dollar Falls 100-101
Monarch Mountain . . .52, 58, 59
Monument Trail 138, 139
Moosehide Village 144, 145
Morel (mushrooms) . . .6, 18, 19
Mosquitos 32
Mount Archibald 113
Mount Barker 102, 105
Mt Chester Henderson . .150-151
Mount Decoeli 90, 112-113
Mount Distincta . . .128, 156-157
Mount Granger 70, 172
Mount Haldane 128
Mount Hare 160, 161
Mount Hoge 122, 126
Mount Ingram 68-69
Mount Jeckyll 159
Mount Logan 15, 90
Mount Lorne 74-75
Mount Lucania 15, 90
Mount McIntyre 70-79
Mount Monolith 146-149
Mount Montana 30, 78-79
Mount Robert Henderson 150-151
Mount Ripley 92, 93
Mount Ripinski 94-95
Mount Saint Elias 15, 40
Mount White 52, 56, 57
Mud Bay Loop 92-93

Mush Lake Road 102-104

Nahanni River 46
Nares Mountain 77
North Ogilvie Range 15, 156,-157

Observation Mountain . .114-116

Paddling 46
Parks Canada 184
Peel River 16, 46
Pepper Spray 41
Pine Lake 44, 110-111

Reid Falls 82, 83
Renewable Resources 185
Richardson Range 160-161
Ridge Road Heritage Trail . .128
Ridge Trail 130-131
Riverdale 60, 62, 64
Robert Cambell Highway 21
Rock Glacier Trail 100-101
Ross River 178-180
Running 44

Saint Elias Lake 100-101
Salmon 20
Sapper Hill 158, 159
Samuel Glacier 90, 98-99
Seasons 33
Seven Mile Saddle 94-95
Sheep/ Bullion Plateau . .118-119
Sheep Mountain area 90, 118-119
Shorty Creek 102, 105
Silver Basin Trail 130, 139
Silver Trail 136-139, 165
Skagway . .2, 53, 82-88, 178-180
Skiing 48-49
Ski-joring 48-49
Slims RiverValley . .90, 114-117
Snowboarding 48-49
Soldiers Summit 120-121

Sourdough Hill 138-139
South Ogilvie Range 15, 146-155
Spruce Beetle Trail 110-111
Sternwheeler Graveyard .142-143
Sturgills Landing 82-83
Summit Mountain .152, 154-155
Swan Haven 21
Swimming 44

Tagish 52
Tagish Road 52
Takini Hot Springs 44
Takini River 46
Tatshensheni River 46, 189
Tatshensheni Park 90, 91
Teslin 2, 178,-180
Three Guardsman Road . . .96-97
Thundereggs 91
Thunderegg Creek 110, 111
Tombstone Mountain . . .146-149
Tombstone Pass 148-149
Trans-Canada Trail 50

Upper Tanana 24-27

Wade Mountain 112-125
Watson Lake 2
Wye Lake 54-55
Whitehorse . .2, 52, 60, 178-180
Whitehorse Fishladder 60-61
Whitehorse Walkway 60-61
White Pass 52, 53, 80, 81
Williscroft Canyon 120-121
Wright Pass 160
Wolfe Creek 62-63

Yukon Conservation Society .173
Yukon River 16, 46

ABOUT THE AUTHOR

Ed Vos

Curtis Vos was born and raised in Kingston, Ontario. In the early nineties he made his way up to the North and has been there ever since.

In addition to this book Curtis is the author and illustrator of Klondike Ho, a cartoon history of the great goldrush.

This book is the result of a three year odyssey of research, field work and design, done between bush work and odd jobs.

Curtis Vos lives in a cabin near Whitehorse with his two dogs and is presently working on a follow up to this book; The Yukon Naturalism Guide, an introduction to the plants, animals and geography of the Territory.